MW01254874

The Kuřim Case

A Terrifying True Story of Child Abuse, Cults & Cannibalism

Ryan Green

© **Copyright 2016 by Ryan Green**
All rights Reserved.

ISBN-13: 978-1535024389
ISBN-10: 1535024380

Table of Contents

Acknowledgments 5

Introduction... 6

Chapter 1 – Abuse Uncovered 8

    Upbringings and Pasts..16

    Setting Upon the Path to Recovery................................. 28

Chapter 2 – Now you see her... 33

    Connecting the Dots...37

    The Horrifying Full Extent of the Abuse 43

    Guessing at the Motives.. 45

Chapter 3 – The Journey of a Thousand Miles 51

    At the heart of winter 52

    Homecoming.. 56

Chapter 4 – The trial.. 64

    Tying all the knots... 64

    Events according to Klára Mauerová's testimony 68

    Turek testifies..73

    The Barbora question..75

    Psychiatrists' findings 77

Chapter 5 – The trial, continued 82

    A third opinion 86

    Closing statements 87

    Final words.. 90

Verdicts and sentences...91

Unsolved mysteries and unanswered questions 92

Conclusion – The aftermath **94**

About the Author.. **98**

Other Titles by Ryan Green... **99**

Acknowledgments

I want to say a big thank you to Helen Green, Lacar Musgrove, Prints Magoncia, James Sibbet, Michaela Kucerova and Linda Avellino. I couldn't have done it without you.
~Ryan

Introduction

Motherhood is amongst the most precious and revered of roles in human society. Through the ages and across species, the bond between mother and child has been sacred; and even while, with the changing of times and modernisation of society it becomes less popular or mandatory as a life goal, it still retains an almost mystical charm. If a woman has decided to weather the years of highs and lows that come with nurturing and caring for a child, there is an expectation – that she possesses a deep tenderness and care for the child unrivalled by any other, and will do anything to protect them from suffering and harm. That capacity, meant to be written into our genes, most of the time can be relied upon as surely as the world turns.

But sometimes – more times than is comfortable to think about – something goes wrong. That capacity gets subverted, inverted, or erased altogether, and rather than fulfilling the role of protector, a mother becomes that very one who inflicts suffering and pain upon her offspring.

In May of 2007, in a small, quiet town in the South Moravia region of the Czech Republic, a technical glitch – a simple, accidental crossing of signals – revealed just such a case, and an entire nation watched transfixed with horror as the grisly extent of the perversion of the maternal instinct was revealed. Two small brothers named Jakub and Ondrej, nine and seven years old respectively, were revealed to have suffered confinement, mutilation, psychological brutality, and cannibalism at the hands of several people – foremost among them their own mother and her sister.

The ensuing investigation and trial captivated the country as a web of secrecy and manipulation was laid bare. That entire nation's attention was transfixed as the disappearance of a teenage girl revealed a daring case of concealed identity and international intrigue, culminating in a thousand-mile chase in the depths of a Scandinavian winter.

The allegations that were levelled would keep any parent of a young child awake at night. A secretive cult operating in close proximity to children: stealing, forging medical records, and possibly attempting to create a new messiah was in full swing. All the while its members appeared, on the surface, to be models of excellent caregivers.

This is the story of the infamous 'Kuřim Case', an investigation that engrossed the public and media of a whole country for two years. It is a story of intense cruelty and sadism, inflicted on the most vulnerable members of society; if you are especially sensitive to accounts of the suffering of children, you may find it advisable not to read any farther. If, however, you seek to understand the darker side of human nature by coming face to face with it, then this book is written for you.

Through the testimony of the victims, the perpetrators and other witnesses and analysis from experts and psychiatrists who examined the case and those involved in it, delve inside to learn what happened, why it happened, and what ripple effects propagated into the future.

Chapter 1 – Abuse Uncovered

The story begins in Kuřim, a tiny town of around 10,000 inhabitants in the region of South Moravia, about 9 miles North-West of Brno, which is the second largest city in the Czech Republic. Like all small towns that lie in the shadow of a big city, Kuřim is relatively quiet and subdued, without much big business and commerce. Most of its infrastructure is low-density residential and houses, mostly single-storey, dominate the architecture, with the occasional block of flats rising no more than a few storeys high. Aside from a church and a castle – the former dating back to the 13th century and the latter in the 15th – there isn't much in the way of sightseeing to be done in Kuřim. The most interesting things that happen on any average day are the morning and evening rush as people from the town and further out make their way to and from their jobs in the larger city.

On a Monday morning in early May 2007, a discovery was made that would go on to shatter the peace and relative obscurity the town had previously enjoyed, and its reputation would henceforth be one no settlement would want to be associated with.

On the morning of the 7th May, a new father tested a baby monitor of the type that relays video, which he had bought several months previously. His name was Eduard Trdý, and his wife had just gone into labour earlier that morning. She was giving birth to their first child. One can easily imagine his excitement and anticipation as he unboxed the baby monitor, thinking about the child that he would soon be nurturing.

As he switched the screen on, he received a bit of a surprise. Rather than the interior of his own house, what appeared was an image he considered at first as just odd: a small naked boy he did not recognise, looking to be perhaps six or seven years of age, his hands bound up and playing with a roll of Scotch tape.

The image was grainy monochrome. The camera sending the signal was operating in extremely low-light or near-complete darkness, and he could see just enough to discern that it was a small room.

Clearly, this was the result of a glitch, the monitor picking up the signal of a nearby set of the same type. Perhaps distracted by his impending parenthood, Trdý didn't immediately connect the scene in front of him with abuse. The boy didn't look miserable – rather, he seemed quite content with his improvised toy. Maybe he was just playing in his favourite little space, perhaps pretending to be in a bunker or secret enchanted room, as little boys sometimes do.

Trdý went on with his day. At 5 o'clock that evening, following a visit to his wife and child in the maternity ward, he revisited the invading video stream once again. The boy was still in the little room. Surely if he was just playing he wouldn't still be in there after six whole hours – children don't usually have that much patience with any one game. This time, though, the image that confronted him was more disturbing: the boy was still tied up and was eating something off the floor.

"Zůstal jsem sedět jako opařený" ["I was shocked"], Trdý later recounted to the press. He had spent about a quarter of an hour puzzling over the footage on his screen, trying to discern whether it was real or not. Eventually, Trdý decided that whatever it was, it was worth letting the police know about it. Just in case he lost the feed before they arrived, he recorded the footage.

The police arrived not long after, and after looking at the footage, they decided to investigate. Miroslav Gregor, the leading officer at the scene, made a few quick deductions in his head: baby monitors are usually designed to transmit to a receiver within the same premises. *"Předpokládali jsme, že zařízení má malý dosah"* ["We figured that the baby monitor would have had short range"] he later recounted, *"Že může být maximálně ve vedlejším domě."* ["That it couldn't have been further than next door."]

None of the immediate neighbours, when questioned, admitted to having a small boy in a dark room somewhere on their property. One of the doors they knocked on was that of Klára Mauerová, a 29-year-old woman who had moved in about half a year earlier, in December of 2006. Klára was a reclusive woman, and aside from the occasional glimpses, had hardly been seen by her neighbours since moving to Kuřim.

When asked if there was a little boy anywhere in their house, she said no. The only child in the house was her thirteen-year-old daughter Anička, who was ill and would be upset by strangers bumbling around the house. Out of politeness and the fact that they had no solid reason to believe she was hiding anything, the officers excused themselves.

Fortunately, Eduard Trdý was still in his house watching and recording the view on the monitor. Through it, he had heard the conversation Gregor had had with Klára and immediately replayed the footage for him when he returned. Hearing the words he had traded with Klára playing back to him it was enough for Gregor to press Klára for a search. On top of that he could actually recognise the song that had been playing rather loudly over the radio in her house.

This time, Klára could not object to the search – her house was now considered an active crime scene. Gregor and his two colleagues entered and began to investigate. The girl Klára had said was her adolescent daughter reacted badly indeed, screaming loudly upstairs as the police searched the ground floor. The sweep revealed one possibility for the room in Trdý's monitor: a padlocked door that looked like it led into a closet or small room under the staircase.

Gregor and his colleagues asked Klára to open the door for them, and she answered that she could not. She had found the door locked herself when she moved into the place, she told them, and the landlord had never given her the key. That wasn't going to be a problem – the fire department was called in. They were through the lock in no time.

Just as the police had called in their reinforcements, Klára had called in her own: her sister Kateřina, who was two years her senior. As the fire department arrived with their cutting tools, the two of them, joined by the thirteen-year-old Anička sat down in front of the door, obstructing the firefighters from accessing it.

Anička – the Czech diminutive form of her proper name Ana – was herself a sight to behold: dressed in a red and yellow patterned dress, with round glasses and a cap on her head, at a glance she appeared to be an adolescent. But she behaved like a much younger child – she came down to join her mother and aunt crawling on all fours, babbling and rocking herself like an infant. She seemed to be developmentally challenged in some way.

The police and firefighters had no choice but to physically remove the three of them from the door. Klára and Kateřina made a few haphazard attempts to resist but were quickly overpowered. Ana, on the other hand, put up a fight. As soon as responders laid hands on her, she got up and began kicking, hitting, and scratching at them. Tomáš Kotrhonz, one of the police officers who had to deal with Ana, bore the brunt of her attacks and described them as weak even for her age. Since she was a child, Kotrhonz and his colleagues did not respond to her aggression in kind, putting it down to her trying to defend her mother. Once they had prised her away, she ran crying "mama, mama!" – Oddly not to her supposed mother, but to her aunt Kateřina.

With their obstacle cleared, the firefighters made short work of the lock and opened the door. The first thing to hit everyone at the scene was the smell – the smell of months' worth of human excretions. All over the bare concrete floor was the source of the smell: vomit, human excrement, and dried urine. It was the beginning of summer, and the heat in the little room was unbearable.

Instantly drawing the eyes, though, was the small, pale, naked figure sitting calmly in the middle of all the filth: the little boy from Eduard Trdý's baby monitor.

Despite his extreme discomfort, the squalor of his surroundings, or the sudden tumult he had been thrust into, the boy did not cry. Klára identified him as her son Ondrej. When she was asked why she was keeping her son like this, Kotrhonz recalled, *"Klára Mauerová nám řekla, že tomu nerozumíme, že to nemůžeme pochopit."* [Klára Mauerová said that we didn't get it, that we couldn't have possibly understood].

She was so distraught, emotional, and incoherent that no information of value could be extracted from her.

From Kateřina, on the other hand, they got something approximating an explanation. According to her, Eduard Trdý's first impression upon seeing the little boy on his screen was close to the truth. The little room under the stairs reminded Ondrej of the one Harry Potter lived in at his uncle and aunt's house, and so became his favourite spot to play in. About the sparseness and filth of the room, or why Ondrej had to be naked and tied up while "playing," no explanation was given.

Paramedics were called to the scene, but first the police had to take a photograph of the crime scene in the state in which it was found before they could help him. When the camera was brought in and pointed at him, little Ondrej did something that would cause the heart of anyone with a shred of decency and any kind of deductive capability to sink. Still bound up as he was, he looked straight into the camera and smiled.

Scars, seen and unseen

Ondrej was whisked away in an ambulance. His apparent nonchalance at the situation persisted – his demeanour reflected nothing worse happening to him than a fall from a bicycle, as medics described. Things changed when bedtime came after his arrival at the hospital, though, and the psychological trauma he bore began to manifest. He became delirious and extremely fearful, thinking the pictures on the wall were ghosts. The pictures had to be taken down, but this gave him little comfort. His sleep was riven with nightmares. Nurses tried their best to comfort him as he trembled and pleaded, "Just kill me. Please just kill me."

Immediately visible on Ondrej were physical marks that looked deliberate: long scars on his arms and back that could have been the result of slashes with sharp objects. Peculiar pale welts in his groin area. A largish circular scar on his buttocks. These details were initially suppressed in official statements made to the press, saying he was treated for dehydration and keeping mum on the rest.

Ondrej had a brother two years older than him named Jakub. Jakub had been at school during the bust, mercifully spared the specific ordeal that his little brother had been subjected to. Ondrej had not been at school because of a diagnosis of hearing problems that ostensibly made learning in a classroom environment difficult for him, hence his being pulled out of school, supposedly to be home-schooled by his mother.

With his legal caregiver in police custody, Jakub was taken to the Brno Children's Institution, soon joined by Anička. Although he was distressed and disoriented at the sudden change and not knowing where his mother was, the authorities had to try to get any information from him that could might shed light on what had been going on at home.

They achieved little success: he seemed extremely reluctant to speak – more, even than a child in the company of strangers would be expected to. He avoided all eye contact, keeping his attention fixed on the book he had been given to keep him occupied. Examinations of his body showed scars similar to those Ondrej's, with the exception of the large one on the buttocks.

Jakub said the scars were the result of scratches from a pet gerbil, the odd welts in his groin area wasp stings received while camping. Neither explanation seemed likely, and when caregivers pressed him gently for the truth, he finally divulged that they had been inflicted by his mother. The scratches were from a fork dragged forcefully against his skin, the welts from cigarettes being put out on his groin. She had never been a smoker, he said – she had bought the cigarettes only for the purpose of burning him and his younger brother with them.

As a few days passed, the initial shock of the drastic change waned, and they began to speak more freely and openly. According to Ondrej, the confinement had begun near the end of the previous summer. When the family moved into the Kuřim house in December of 2006, he had at first been confined in the bathroom before being transferred to the under-stairs closet, and the only time he had been in the living room of the house had been Christmas day. Other than that, his entire existence had been that of a prisoner in solitary confinement in a particularly brutal prison. He had eaten his meals in the darkness, and he had had to urinate and defecate in a bucket.

Both boys also mentioned a third adult they had frequent contact with – someone they called "Aunt Nenci." According to Jakub, Aunt Nenci worked at a day-care centre both he and Ondrej had attended, and she also walked him to and from school. Ondrej claimed to have been confined in a room at said day-care centre before the move to Kuřim. During which time Aunt Nenci had watched over him and given him food.

A little detective work revealed Aunt Nenci to be Hana Bašova, a social worker and formal colleague of Kateřina. The day-care centre – which was named "Paprška", meaning "(Light)Beam" – was, in fact where the two had worked together. Upon determining her identity, police brought Bašova in for questioning. She denied noticing anything wrong, and when the alleged confinement at the day-care centre was brought up, she put it down to a simple misunderstanding on Ondrej's part – what he had described was a punishment room children were sent to for a "time-out" when they misbehaved, the significance of which had probably been exaggerated in his young mind.

Lacking probable cause, hard evidence, or reliable testimony, the police did not make a move to arrest her at that time.

Ana

The boys slowly opened up, but Ana proved more difficult to handle. Everyone who encountered her was convinced she had developmental challenges, and she seemed especially upset by the separation from her adoptive mother. Employees at the Institution had a difficult time even getting close to her, and she would raise raucous hell, fighting, biting and screaming every time anyone tried to touch her. It was likely that examinations of her body would turn up evidence of deliberate scarification, but her behaviour made it impossible to do so. Social workers decided to leave her be for a while and allow her to get accustomed to her new surroundings before trying to examine her or even give her a bath.

They would never get the chance to do this: early on the 12th May, three days after the bust, Anička disappeared from the Institution. It appeared she had figured out how to open one of the windows and climbed out. No one could determine whether she had escaped on her own or had been aided by somebody. Neither prospect was palatable: either there was a mentally challenged girl alone and lost in the woods nearby, or she had been whisked away by co-

conspirators or participants in the torture of the boys. If the latter was the case, whatever they had planned for her was not likely to be good.

They had to find her and find her quickly before she slipped out of their grasp completely. If she had been taken away by some adult and that abductor had also been involved in the torture, they must be captured and brought to justice. Authorities immediately ordered a high-priority search, beginning with a sweep of the woods using infrared goggles, the canine unit, and DNA from items of clothing. The sweep of the forest failed to locate her, as did door-to-door enquiries in the surrounding neighbourhood. With no trace of her to be found close to the Children's Institution, the probability that she had been aided in her escape by an adult seemed all the more likely.

Upbringings and Pasts

I've dealt in previous books with how the roots of the pathologies that led to my subjects' crimes lay at least partly in their childhoods. In all of them thus far, that connection has been variable but convincing. This case defies that pattern: there is no indication that significant trauma in Klára or Kateřina's childhoods influenced their actions.

Kateřina was the firstborn daughter of Ladislav and Eliška Mauerová, and Klára their youngest. In the middle is another sister, Gabriela. The family was very tight-knit, going on frequent outings and holidays together, often with their extended family. They were moderately religious Catholics, occasionally going to church, but Ladislav and Eliška made sure to raise them on the principles of the Ten Commandments and the Golden Rule.

With this loving environment, the sisters were very good friends growing up. Kateřina and Gabriela were more bookish and heavily invested in their academics, while Klára was more active and sporty, fulfilling that passion with volleyball, gymnastics, and synchronised swimming.

Klára's early motherhood and marriage

In 1996, at the age of 18, Klára had an unplanned pregnancy with Radek Coufal, with whom she had been in a relationship with for a year. The pair married not long after the pregnancy was discovered. In October of 1997, they had their first child, whom they named Jakub. Two years later, in September 1999, they had Ondrej.

Mothers who have unplanned children at a young age often have a hard time with life afterwards, but Klára was fortunate: she and the father of her son were in a stable relationship, and her parents were also thrilled and proud at finally becoming grandparents. They offered all the help they could, including allowing Klára and Coufal to live with them for the first year of their marriage until they could afford their own apartment. Buoyed by so much support, Klára attained a degree in economics and embarked on a secretarial career.

Klára and Gabriela remained close as they grew older. Gabriela recalled Klára as having been an excellent mother. *"Byla výborná maminka a pro mě vzor. Říkala jsem si, že bych jednou chtěla mít se svými dětmi taky takový vztah"* ["She was a great mother and I admired her. I wished that in the future I'd have the same relationship with my own children"], Gabriela later fondly recalled. Klára had never exhibited any inclination to or tolerance of violence, and her family and those who knew her closely found it difficult to stomach the recent revelations.

Klára's marriage did not last very long – neighbours reported that she and Coufal began to have heated arguments in 2003. Their disagreements continued to mount until the relationship reached its breaking point, and by the end of the year Coufal had moved out and begun divorce proceedings.

The couple's separation was amicable. Neither party placed any fault on the other. Time had simply revealed differences in opinion between the two of them.

The boys remained in the custody of their mother, and Coufal did not contest this as he, too, had utmost faith in Klára's fitness for motherhood. Their relationship remained amicable, and Coufal continued to play an active role in his sons' lives, providing for them as Klára requested and spending all the time he could with them, taking them to sports practice sessions, outings, and the like.

The Arrival of Ana

In 2004, Klára decided to follow Kateřina's footsteps and began studying social childcare and education. A year later, another significant change occurred in Klára's life – she gained a daughter in the form of Anička. To friends and neighbours looking from the outside, the change was as surprising as it was sudden. She had never talked about wanting to adopt, nor had they heard anything from her about the necessarily long and intricate legal process she had no doubt gone through to attain the adoption. Neighbours in her block of flats in Brno had only seen the occasional glimpse of Ana – a pale, sickly child who was often carried up and down the stairs as if she couldn't navigate them herself. Her arrival had also heralded a change in Klára – she became increasingly hard-pressed for time, refused any company coming over to her flat, and always seemed exhausted and sad.

Marcela Zednickova, a friend of Klára's, was probably the only one of her friends to spend any considerable length of time close to Anička. Her sons were about the same age as Jakub and Ondrej, and they went on many outings together, their boys keeping each other company while the two of them were left to chat. It was on the last outing they had together, to see a movie, that she met the child. Klára didn't say much about her, and Marcela couldn't help but notice her odd behaviour, staring at the ground through the entire movie and steadily avoiding any contact with her or anyone other than Klára. When Marcela asked Klára about this odd behaviour, Klára replied that Anička was autistic and heavily averse to contact with strangers. Soon after that trip, Klára grew more and more distant until they stopped meeting and she began ignoring phone calls.

Klára's ex-husband also knew very little about Anička or what had driven Klára to adopt her. He did occasionally catch sight of her when he was picking up or dropping off the boys but never probed Klára about her. Klára herself didn't volunteer much information, and Coufal wasn't going to press her for what he saw as her own business. If she wasn't telling him anything, she probably had her reasons for doing so, and he respected the fact that they now led separate lives.

Anička's adoption was approved and recognised by the state. The authorities, therefore, did know a lot more about her. According to her adoption documents, the account given by Klára and her family was that little Anička was the daughter of drug addicts who were known to Antonia Drčmanová, mother to Eliška Mauerová and grandmother to Klára, Kateřina and Gabriela. Because of her developmental problems, Anička's parents were overwhelmed by her care, a situation exacerbated by the challenges they faced with the demon of addiction. Touched by the plight of the innocent child born into such a difficult situation, Antonia would occasionally care for Anička during the day and make sure she was fed and clothed.

One day in 2000, Anička's parents dropped her off with Antonia as usual, but they never returned to pick her up. Antonia tried but failed to locate them. Perhaps they had come to some grievous harm during the course of the day but just as likely, they may have decided to run away from one of their problems and relocated somewhere else, believing that Antonia would take care of Anička and perhaps telling themselves that removing themselves from the child's life would be the best thing for her.

The story goes that Antonia took Anička in and took care of her until she passed away in 2004. Klára then took over as her caregiver and soon began the process of formally adopting her. Since Anička was completely undocumented, the process was especially complicated. Fortunately, a friend of Kateřina's – a journalist named Jakub Patočka – was an activist who frequently advocated for people seeking adoptions and was well versed in the system.

With Patočka's help, Klára managed to clear every hurdle, which included court appearances and evaluations by social workers, a DNA sequencing of Anička, and an oath-bound testimony about the veracity of this account from Klára's mother Eliška.

In October 2006, Klára withdrew from her studies citing serious personal and family difficulties, not long before Ana's adoption was finalised and the family moved to Kuřim – during which time the abuse of her two sons had already started. The tragedy of Ana's story and the increased pressure Klára came under after taking her in could go a long way towards explaining the change in her demeanour and pulling away from her social circles. If she had become unsociable since Anička had appeared in her life, the move to Kuřim heralded an even more drastic withdrawal. Previous friends were almost completely cut off, and she never gave so much as a greeting to her new neighbours.

Her family also received the same treatment. As involved as they had been in their grandchildren's upbringing, Eliška and Ladislav Mauerová were told they could no longer see them. According to Ladislav, the reason they were given was that the boys were beginning to exhibit behavioural problems, and that the root was an inappropriate fixation with their grandparents. *"Dcera si chtěla zvýšit respekt a autoritu u kluků"* ["Our daughter just wanted to gain more respect and authority with the boys"], he later explained. *"Tak nám řekla, že bude třeba kontakty omezit."* ["And so she told us we would need to limit the contact with them."] Gabriela, who had been very close with her younger sister, found herself ignored and cut out of her life.

As late as the first couple of months of the summer of 2006, the boys' father had been taking them to their practice sessions and visiting them on weekends, but things changed in late July of that year. The weekend visits were cut supposedly because of an educational program involving outings to observe animals in their natural habitat. Following that, if he ever managed to see them it was only from afar, and he never got to spend any significant amount of time with them until Ondrej was found languishing in the closet.

The only person who did not receive the cut-off treatment from Klára was her eldest sister, Kateřina. Even though Klára looked up to her, the two of them had never been particularly close. After Klára took in Anička, they became closer. It appeared that Klára had turned to Kateřina and her expertise in childcare to help her deal with the change in her life, and when the move to Kuřim was made, Kateřina moved in with them. After that, Kateřina was the only person whose company Klára regularly kept.

An Eerie Child

Knowing this "official history" of Klára and her family allows us to make a few speculations: Ana's appearance in Klára's life seems to have put a great deal of pressure on her. Taking care of a child is not an easy thing, and when that child is as mentally handicapped as Ana seems to have been, things become exponentially harder. Klára also still had her two biological children to worry about – perhaps she found herself overwhelmed, leading her out of desperation to put Ondrej away somewhere she could just forget about him, and when the stress became too much, she had also physically taken it out on both boys – and perhaps Ana, as well.

As investigators took a closer look, certain things about Ana began to seem somewhat out of place. In order to calm her down following the discovery of Ondrej's situation and the disruption it caused, she had been provided with a pencil and paper to doodle on. The doodles she had made surprised the caregivers at the Institution: strings of binary – the base-two mathematical system that underlies the deep inner workings of all our computers – covered the page. Along with them was a calculus formula, the cube-root of nine and two drawings of representations of a tesseract (a four-dimensional cube), one intact, and one an "exploded" view of how it would look in three dimensions.

Complex as these concepts are even for an adult, Ana's knowledge of them could still be explained. It is a well-known fact that people with autism often have phenomenal faculties of recall and mathematical aptitude, and Ana could have been just such a child.

The photographs that were released of her opened up an intriguing new avenue of inquiry. Friends and co-workers of the accused were just as transfixed by the case as everyone else, and several co-workers of Kateřina's noticed something: Ana looked a whole lot like someone they knew – a woman by the name of Barbora Škrlová, whom they had all worked with and who had shared an apartment with Kateřina.

Barbora would have been thirty-two years old at that time. Kateřina had known her since the two of them were in university, where she had studied musical composition. Later on, it had been Kateřina who hired her at the day-care. None of their colleagues had seen Barbora in a long time – she had stopped working at the day-care centre due to illness some years previously. Right around 2005, in fact. She had been rather plump but lost an astonishing amount of weight just prior to ceasing to come to work.

Presented with this information, caregivers at the Institution came forward with an observation they had found odd but had not thought was especially significant: in their interactions with Ana, many of them came away with the impression that she was older than her claimed thirteen years. Her eyes were the greatest source of suspicion – her gaze seemed far too mature for an adolescent. She also had stretch marks – highly unusual for a girl of her age, although still plausible if she had suffered very rapid weight loss. In hindsight some of them admitted that she could have been much older, but they still defended their lack of alarm by the fact that any of the anomalies they had observed in Ana could have been the result of illness, extremely vigorous medical treatments, or trauma. When Kateřina was questioned about whether Ana was in fact Barbora, she put it down as ludicrous – she had known both Barbora and Ana, and they were definitely two distinct people.

The entire nation was spellbound by this intriguing new possibility, and as the police conducted their inquiry, there were efforts in the public sphere to unravel the mystery of where Ana had disappeared to as well as where she had originated. A popular national tabloid offered a bounty of 100,000 Czech Koruna, about £2,400 at the time, for anyone who could provide information on her whereabouts, and one of the nation's private TV stations even brought in a psychic to prognosticate on the case, an obvious publicity stunt was of no help.

A Grieving Mother's Hope

Meanwhile in Krnov, the town bordering the Polish border where grandmother Antonia Drčmanová had lived and Ana had supposedly originated, the doubt now cast over Ana's identity gave lent hope of solving a tragic mystery from nearly a decade earlier. In 1996, a father named Jaroslav Sysalov was convicted of the murder of his four-year-old daughter, Karolina. Jaroslav was at the time divorced from Karolina's mother. The little girl had disappeared while he was spending time with her. According to him, he had been on a drive with her when he was knocked unconscious by unseen assailants while the vehicle was stationary, and that when he had awakened, he found his daughter gone.

The courts found his explanation implausible, and he was convicted and sentenced to thirteen years' imprisonment for her murder, even though no body was found. When the possibility that this mystery child with a dubious origin was not who her caregivers said she was came up, Karolina's mother Bohdana came forward with the hope that maybe, just maybe, her ex-husband was innocent after all and Ana was her long-lost daughter.

There were a few inconsistencies – Karolina would have been fifteen by the year 2007, while Ana's claimed age was thirteen, but since there was no official documentation of Ana before her adoption, it was still possible that her age was a fabrication meant to throw off any inquirers who might have suspected the connection. There was also the fact that Ana was apparently autistic, while Karolina had been a healthy and communicative child. Autism typically manifests symptoms earlier than the age of four, though in extremely rare instances, it has appeared later. The other, more horrifying, possibility is that the child suffered enough torture to break her mentally and had been socially deprived to the point that she manifested autism-like symptoms.

Ana Sends a Letter

A few days after Bohdana Sysalová made her hopeful claim, the press and the Premier Ombudsman of South Moravia received a handwritten letter . Its alleged sender was Ana. It offered an explanation for why she had run away from the institution – she had seen the news of her mother's arrest on one of the televisions in the Institution and become so distraught she felt she had to find and help her.

The Institution did all it could to ensure the children were shielded from anything pertaining to the case, making sure they had no access to newspapers

24

and vigilantly watching over what they saw on the TV. This was difficult, given the massive media storm that surrounded the case from the very moment news about it broke. One of the caregivers admitted to having left Ana unattended in front of a TV while they went to the toilet, during which time Ana could have fiddled around with it until she came across a station that was covering the story.

The letter also attempted to explain why Ondrej had been locked up in the closet. It was a harsh punishment, but according to the letter, one which the little boy deserved. He was wildly unruly, it said, and would threaten to kill both her and their mother. Klára had initiated the punishment to try to work his bad tendencies out of him.

The letter was met with scepticism. Even on the surface it was dubious. It was supposedly written by a mentally challenged thirteen-year-old, and it was a full ten pages long, with no mistakes crossed out or significant errors in grammar and spelling. Its vocabulary and cadence were childlike, but certain parts of it exposed a degree of experience in the writer that no child could have. Its handwriting did, however, match that on the doodles Ana had left behind. If it had been written by her, then it had to have been done so with the guidance of an adult who could have dictated the details or censored certain information.

Another oddity in the letter was that it used only male pronouns, indicating the writer experienced some form of gender dysphoria. At that moment, curiosity hinted at one of the more bizarre turns this case would take in the coming months. The letter was eventually traced to a scout cottage in the woods – one at which Kateřina and Barbora Škrlová had worked. When the cottage was searched, it was found empty. If Ana and her helpers had been there, they had long abandoned it.

A Questionable Adoption

One of the adults who had come to visit following the three children's rescue was Jakub Patočka, the activist who had helped Ana get adopted. He presented himself as a concerned party, owing to his involvement in Ana's adoption. With the difficult time they were having in communicating with her, caregivers at the institution welcomed the possibility that he could possibly get through to her as one of the few people she was likely to be familiar with and whom they were confident was not involved in the abuse. He didn't succeed, but was present when she threw a tantrum demanding to get on the phone with her adoptive mother, to which the resident psychiatrist had acquiesced.

It was a couple of days after that that Ana disappeared, and the police had subsequently reassessed the role they thought he had played. The extent of his involvement in the adoption itself was unknown, and if there had been any doubt about Ana's true identity it was possible that he involved. If that were the case, giving him access to Ana had been a mistake. Perhaps he had used that opportunity to secretly give her instructions for breaking out; he could even have been the person who aided her in her escape.

Pursuing this line of inquiry, the police raided Patočka's apartment in Brno and searched it looking for any trace of Ana or any evidence that could shed light on her identity – some official record, perhaps, or a piece of correspondence. They came up empty handed on both counts. There wasn't even a trace that matched the DNA they had sequenced from the samples recovered from the Institution, so it was unlikely that she had passed through his house on the way to somewhere else.

When questioned, Patočka maintained that if there was any deception, he had been neither part of it nor aware of it. He had only communicated with his old acquaintance Kateřina, and had only seen Ana once throughout the entire adoption process. Besides her apparent mental challenges, he had seen nothing out of the ordinary in her, nor did the way she behaved with Klára and Kateřina point to any fear of either of them that might have indicated she was being abused. He had acted in good faith throughout the entire process, seeing no reason to distrust the information he was being given by the Mauerová sisters. He still expressed his trust in them even after the abuse of Klára's two sons came to light, saying that he wanted to do all he could to help them through their trying time.

If Ana were indeed not who she was claimed to be, especially if she were much older than her apparent age, Patočka could be added to the long list of people who had been fooled. Police officers and firefighters had seen nothing amiss, and even experts in childcare had been unable to detect anything that raised enough flags to convert slight unease into alarm. If Patočka really had been fooled, he revealed that this impression had stretched back all the way to around the time of the custody hearing.

The fact that Ana had been legally adopted raised some questions about the hearing itself: the legal system is supposed to apply utmost scrutiny to any case that passes through it. To be adopted, Ana had to have passed through that scrutiny, which opened a myriad of questions: how could that have been possible? Had the Mauerová sisters' powers of deception been that good, or had the officials who oversaw the adoption overlooked something or perhaps even colluded? Jaroslava Rezova, the judge who had presided over the case, maintained that she had seen a child in her courtroom – and she had had two and a half hours in her presence, so she was absolutely sure.

The squaring of this particular circle came courtesy of the DNA that had been sequenced from the samples collected from the Institution: whoever the "Ana" who had been recovered from Kateřina's house was, she was not the same person as the one who had been present in that courtroom. The DNA sample that had been taken from that girl during the adoption process did not match the one they had on hand.

Speculation once again ran rampant in the public's imagination: could the girl in the courtroom have been the real Ana, and if so, what had happened to her? Had something terrible happened to her – accidental death, perhaps, prompting the Mauerová sisters to go to desperate measures to conceal the fact? Could she still be alive, hidden somewhere and having unspeakable things done to her?

Investigators were pursuing another angle with the case: they had noticed another link between Kateřina and Barbora Škrlová beyond studying and working together: Barbora had been part of a religious sect headed by her father, who was named Josef Škrla. The sect was an offshoot of an international religious movement known as the Grail Movement, and Barbora had converted Kateřina to its beliefs, probably sometime during their university years.

The investigators saw this as more than just a coincidental connection – perhaps it had quite a lot to do with the case and the motivations behind it. Consequently, they began with a few inquiries into other members of the sect, and this is where they hit pay dirt: the DNA sample taken in the courtroom was found to belong to the daughter of one Viktor Skála, an actor from Brno and member of the sect. It had been her who had been presented to the court as Ana, eliminating any possibility of the court's extremely thorough examinations finding anything amiss. Not long after that, the one suspicion that had seemed least likely was confirmed: the DNA sample taken from the Institution did, in fact, belong to Barbora Škrlová.

Setting Upon the Path to Recovery

While the drama was playing out in the outside world, the boys, now removed from the abusive environment, were slowly settling into the new regime. Both of them had clearly suffered a great deal of mental trauma and would probably bear its consequences for the rest of their lives.

The first person to interact extensively with Jakub after the liberation was Lenka Malhocká, a caregiver at the Children's Institution in Brno. She took Jakub to her apartment for lunch and an afternoon of board games the next day so that she could get his mind off events a little as well as observe his social behaviours. He seemed unable to perform many very simple tasks that should have been well within the abilities of a nine-year-old. He had had trouble dressing himself after taking a bath, putting his clothes on back-to-front before having to be helped into them. His table manners were appalling, and he was unable to eat without making a substantial mess.

Malhocká managed to slowly work her way through the shell Jakub had woven around himself – she uncovered the true provenance of the scars and burn marks on his body. Following the meal, she played Ludo with him, and while he was progressively becoming freer with himself, his ordeal also seemed to have left him with a habit of dishonesty.

Following the terror of the first night out of his prison, Ondrej began to perk up considerably. His demeanour towards strangers was the complete opposite of Jakub's. His confinement had meant that he had never had to maintain secrecy against outsiders, so he hadn't developed the guardedness his older brother showed. If anything, captivity had left him with a deep longing for human contact. He was friendly and trusting with everyone, chatting with nurses and sitting in their laps even though they were strangers to him. The aspects of freedom that excited him were not what would be expected from a child – rather than access to toys, he seemed fascinated by hygiene products, commenting on how great the toothpaste was, or on how pretty a hairbrush he had been given was.

A lot of the boys' more extreme pathologies cleared up within a few days, but deeper underlying issues remained and flared up with disheartening frequency. The news of the disappearance of Ana, whom they had known as their sister, from the Institution hit them hard. Both of them spoke very protectively and fondly of Ana – she was, in fact, the only person to whom they seemed to have a warm bond of any kind. This appeared innocent enough at first, seeming like the simple fondness of two little boys for someone they had accepted as their sister, but as her true identity was revealed, investigators began to wonder if there was something darker behind it. When the news was broken to them that Ana was not who they thought she was but was instead an impostor, they reacted very badly and were reduced to a terrible psychological state for several days.

The boys' fondness towards Ana seemed to have been developed at the expense of their relationship with each other, a fact that came to light when Ondrej was deemed healthy enough to be discharged from the hospital into the care of the Institution just over a fortnight after his liberation. One would expect their reunion to have been a joyful and enthusiastic affair; instead, it was cold and subdued, as if they had some measure of distrust towards each other. Their relationship would eventually become warmer with time, but during the first few days back together they often broke out into outright hostility.

Family Matters

The rest of the boys' family, who had all been cut out of their lives prior to the abuse being revealed, were eager to resume contact with them. During Ondrej's first few days in hospital, he received a visit from his father, grandparents, and Aunt Gabriela, to which he responded very positively and enthusiastically, bubbling with joy and sharing candy he had been given with all of them.

Naturally, Coufal was eager to have the boys returned to his custody. He had maintained a room for them in his apartment despite Klára's having enforced his isolation from them, and discovering her reasons for doing so had prompted him to go on a redecorating spree, repainting and redecorating the room so that they would have a pleasant atmosphere in which to start over, free from the influences of the past.

However, days turned to weeks without the boys being released into his care, and his frustration built. He found his access to them restricted by the Institution's policies – the times during which he could see them were heavily restricted and extended only to him and not the rest of the family. Out of frustration, both he and the boys' grandparents attempted to get the situation resolved by the courts, but a judge ruled that the decision of whether and when to release them would be left to the Institution. This was not, however a court order giving custody of the boys over to the Institution, and Coufal protested that their continuing to be held in the Institution's care was illegal. Petr Nečas, the Minister of Social affairs, eventually had to weigh in on the matter, saying that the extraordinary nature of this case meant that parental rights could be waived for the wellbeing of the children.

Things eventually got even worse for Coufal and the rest of the family when the Institution decided to revoke visitation rights altogether. It turned out that the Institution extending visitation rights to Coufal, and Coufal alone, was more than just a recommendation. It was a hard and fast rule, and when he violated that rule by bringing other relatives along anyway, they used the implicit power that had been vested in them to ban him from further visits.

As further justification for this decision, the Institution cited the boys' behaviour when in the presence of their extended family members. They became restless and agitated, saying that they were forbidden from speaking, only calming down after they left. This was possibly the result of conditioning by their abusers – Klára, Kateřina, and their accomplices would have been especially vigilant about making sure the boys never let anything slip should

31

they ever be in the presence of the rest of the family. The fact that the boys' reaction was no fault of the family was immaterial – the only thing that mattered was their mental welfare and that they not be exposed to upsetting stimuli.

Another factor in the Institution's wariness to allow visits was that no one could, with complete confidence, be sure that none of the family had been involved in the abuse. The possibility had been entertained from the very beginning, but the debacle with Ana ratcheted the suspicion up even further. The bulk of scrutiny centred on the actions of the boys' grandmother, Eliška Mauerová – she had testified to the veracity of the story of Ana's origins during the adoption hearings. This meant that she was at the very least complicit in the deception – deception committed under oath, no less. Perjury proceedings were pending on her, but the courts did not want to confuse the investigation with additional charges just yet. Investigators had questioned her about it and come away with the impression that she was likely not involved in the abuse itself, but without a hundred percent certainty, the Institution probably decided they were better safe than sorry.

Once again separated from his sons, Coufal began smoking – a habit he had kicked eleven years prior. A couple of weeks later, the court ruled that the Institution had acted beyond its mandate by banning his visits completely, calling it a "gross interference to [his] parental rights and responsibilities." If the visits were actually affecting the boys adversely, the matter should have been decided in the courts.

The decision on who would have ultimate custody over the boys remained unresolved for another four years, long after all of the perpetrators of the abuse had been exposed and brought to justice.

Chapter 2 – Now you see her...

On the 11th June, 2007, Ana Mauerová officially ceased to exist in the eyes of the eyes of the law. At that point, there was no evidence to prove that she had ever existed. No official documents backed her existence, and the person who had been presented as her to the authorities had been proven to be someone else entirely. Numerous eyewitnesses dating back to 2003 had testified to her existence, including some who purported to have known Barbora at the same time, but none of them had had an opportunity to study her closely. Barbora Škrlová had fooled law enforcement and childcare experts, so it was probable that she could have done the same much earlier to Klára's neighbours and family, even while she maintained her true identity to colleagues.

Barbora herself was still missing, and the search for her still had not turned up a single clue as to her whereabouts. Fortunately, it was a few days after the erasure of Ana from official record that she voluntarily reappeared, but in a completely unexpected place. On the 15th June, she turned up seeking a new passport at the Czech embassy in Copenhagen, Denmark, 480 miles away from Brno as the crow flies.

In her company were four men, all Czech nationals: her father, Josef Škrla, a lawyer named Zděnek Hrouzek, a former Czech police officer named Josef Kolinsky, and another man named Vlatislav Ruzička. She had been in the city for a month with relatives who lived there, hiding out of fear of being sent back to the Czech Republic because of the reprisals she might face due to her proximity to the abuse. There was much, much more to the story, they said, and people would not be very kind on her without knowing it.

Kolinsky acted as Barbora's spokesperson to the press. He revealed that she had indeed played the role of Ana, but it had not been for any nefarious purposes. She had done it because deep inside she felt like a child, and she had taken on the persona in order to occupy the "skin" she felt most comfortable in. *"Chtěla být mezi dětmi"* ["She wanted to be among children"], Kolinsky explained, *"protože se jako dítě cítila nejlépe a nejbezpečněji. Jako dospělou osobu ji nikdo nebral vážně. Všichni si z ní dělali legraci a zesměšňovali ji, protože se navenek opravdu chová jako dítě"* ["because as a child she felt happy and safe. She wasn't treated as an adult, no one took her seriously. People laughed at her and made fun of her because of her acting like a child."]

Barbora's behaviour while at the embassy seemed to support this story: she was clutching a teddy bear like a child would. Her personality seemed to slip between that of a person of her actual age and that of a child, begging her father for ice cream or a cake from a bakery they had passed by. Kolinsky also explained her escape from the Institution in very sparse detail: she had hidden in the woods for a while before travelling out of the country by train. There was no explanation of who had helped her, or how she had crossed multiple national borders without a passport.

Since Barbora was not a wanted person at the time, the embassy was powerless to hold her. She and her chaperones left a hair sample for DNA testing and a promise that she would continue to cooperate and remain in contact.

A couple of days later, Czech media and press outlets received a message from Barbora expressing her full willingness to cooperate with the authorities and to testify on every detail that she knew. She also provided a few more details about how she had created the persona of Ana: it had begun while she was working at the daycare centre with Kateřina. She had led a woodcarving group activity and played the piano, and part of the job was naturally supervising the children. That aspect of her work became problematic when she acted more like someone closer to their age than an adult. She had created the persona herself as a way to fit in with the children, hence harmonising her behaviour with what they saw. As the feeling of discomfort with who she was worsened, she sought psychological help to no avail. As a desperate last resort, she turned to her friend Kateřina, who understood and offered to help her assume a new identity.

She also claimed to put to rest the speculation that the entire adoption process had been conducted with an actual child: Viktor Skala's daughter had only been brought in for the DNA test; the rest had been with her. She had sat through psychiatric evaluations by several experts, and all had come away believing she was thirteen years old, one even speculating that she could have been eleven or twelve. All this was presented to the press as proof that her age dysphoria was real, that she could not have been making a show of it. In an interview a few days after that, she stated that "Annie is gone." Oddly, she also spoke about herself – her true identity as Barbora – in third person, indicating some kind of latent dissociation.

Her father had also known a little about the deception, she said, but not much, and had not been involved in it in any way. When asked if she had been assisted by anyone during her escape from the Institution, she refused to divulge any information.

As for Ondrej's incarceration, that had only happened once – on the day of the raid, and he had not been in the closet more than two hours in total. She added on to the story laid out in the letter she had sent from the scout cottage: after receiving light of corporal punishment, Ondrej had screamed that he would kill both her and his brother Jakub. Klára had put him in the closet to cool down and make it known in no uncertain terms that such talk was not to be tolerated in their home.

...Now You Don't

Kolinsky also sent a statement to the media explaining how he had come to be involved with the affair. Josef Škrla, along with Vlatislav Ruzička had visited him when he had become aware that Barbora was in Copenhagen. Ruzička was a business associate of Škrla's but had in a previous career run a secret police unit that planted agents within criminal organisations. He had known Kolinsky outside of their shared work in law enforcement and had recommended that Škrla consult Kolinsky for any additional expertise he could bring. Kolinsky himself recommended that they take the matter to the authorities, arguing that if Barbora was innocent of any wrongdoing, the best way to clear her name was to cooperate with investigators and let them see for themselves.

Prosecutors, however, saw things differently. First of all, their duty was to make sure no wrongdoer in this case was allowed to go free, and the way they perceived Barbora's involvement did not incline them to be charitable towards her. At the time, there was no indication that Barbora had been involved in the abuse, but there was still the fact that she was an adult who had probably witnessed it and yet never made a move to report it. This in itself was a crime, and even if it had happened only once as she said it had, it was her duty to cooperate with the police when they raided the house.

The Brno prosecutor's office made a statement to the press expressing this very sentiment – a move that could charitably be called "inadvisable," considering they were making this proclamation about a person who was not only two national borders away but had also exhibited an impressive propensity to disappear when she wanted to. To compound this, a remarkable amount of time went by without their making any move against her.

Further revelations about Barbora's relationship with Kateřina surfaced: Barbora was at that very time enrolled as a student at Masaryk University in Brno, but the photograph in their records that was purportedly of her was instead that of Kateřina, meaning that Kateřina had quite likely been studying in her name. In light of this possible academic fraud, the university filed a criminal complaint against both of them. The Institution in Brno also had a bone to pick with Barbora. Her duplicity had endangered the safety of the children who were under its care and also tarnished its reputation in the public's eye. The Institution brought a criminal complaint against her for illegal impersonation. It was becoming abundantly clear that Barbora was not likely to walk away from this matter unscathed.

The days continued to tick past. Investigators requested that she be brought back to the Czech Republic so that they could question her more thoroughly, but were rebuffed, her representatives once again citing fear of reprisal. Czech police then enlisted the aid of Interpol to act as their proxies in the questioning. The session was scheduled for the 13th July, nearly a month after Barbora had resurfaced. She failed to show up for the session, and the only person anyone could reach was the lawyer Hrouzek. Citing his impression that the real objective was to get her back to the Czech Republic by force, he would not be pressed to divulge her address, in fact claiming that he did not know it.

The police then expressed their willingness to send someone to Copenhagen to interview her themselves, to which Hrouzek communicated Barbora's compliance before once again withdrawing and saying that the interview could be conducted via Skype. Attempts to schedule the interview came to nothing, and soon Hrouzek himself dropped out of contact, evading any attempts to re-establish it. Barbora had once again disappeared from under the authorities' noses.

Connecting the Dots

Before Barbora's reappearance and subsequent disappearance, the name Josef Škrla had been brought up as a person of interest, in part due to his paternal connection to her. Škrla had an interesting past. Injured by a fall down a flight of stairs in his youth, he had received disability benefit payments for most of his life. This financial safety net had not been enough for him, however: he embarked on a career in "business," though most of his commercial dealings seemed to be obscured in layers of secrecy and outright dishonesty. He was a very convincing salesman, especially good at convincing people to invest in his hidden schemes, only for them to see little or no return.

Few people could say just what he traded in, but it appeared to be connected to international intelligence and military goods. One of his alleged clients was the government of Azerbaijan, and he had been almost responsible for an international incident when that relationship broke down. Škrla had offered the sale of several tanks to the Azerbaijani military in the late 1990s, which offer was turned down. He had then threatened to sell the tanks to Armenia, Azerbaijan's neighbouring country with whom it had a bitter centuries-long rivalry. Škrla had last been seen in the Czech Republic in the early months of that year, and his whereabouts prior to turning up in Denmark with Barbora were not known.

Škrla had also come up due to a peculiar connection that seemed to draw together several principal players in the case. The connection was the religious sect that Škrla led, a splinter of the Grail Movement: his daughter and Klára had belonged to it, as had Viktor Skala, whose daughter had been masqueraded as Ana during the adoption proceedings. It was also found that Hana Bašova, who was closely implicated to the actual abuse in both Jakub and Ondrej's testimony, had also belonged to it.

The venue through which Škrla appeared to have recruited members for his sect was a scout troop he had led in the 1990s, known as Mravenci, which translates to "Ants" in English. Every member of his sect had at some point been a member of the troop.

Followers of the Grail

The mainstream Grail movement is itself a peculiar entity among the tapestry of global religious orders. Its central creed is largely based on a work titled "In

The Light of Truth: The Grail Message," published in 1926 by Oskar Ernst Bernhardt, a German national. It began as a Messianic movement centred around Bernhardt himself – who was known to his followers as Abd-Ru-Shin, meaning "Son of Light" or "Son of the Holy Spirit" depending on who you ask, which was supposedly his name during a previous incarnation in the Levant during the time of Moses.

Today, the movement boasts around ten thousand members worldwide, organised into local "circles" that operate largely independently of each other. Despite his attestations of being the earthly form of "Parsifal Imanuel," the heavenly name of the Messiah, Bernhardt shied away from establishing himself as the central authority of the movement. After his death in 1941, which was explained as his having been recalled back to Heaven by God "as a result of the failure of mankind to such an extent that had not been expected," his message was revised to tone down its Messianic aspects and morphed into the form it currently takes today. The movement still maintains its spiritual epicentre in the Bernhardt family's estate in Vomperberg, Austria, where initiates still make pilgrimages to be baptised.

The Grail Movement already had a varied reputation in the Czech Republic. In 1991, a believer in the Grail Message named Jan Dvorsky had come to the conclusion that Parsifal Imanuel was meant to be reincarnated in order to complete the great work he had left unfinished. After a period of soul-searching, he announced that *he* was the promised reincarnation, publishing his own supplementary creed titled *The Son of Man: The Messiah's Living Word for Restoration of Mankind*. His following did not have an official name but was popularly known as the "Imanuelité" or Imanuelites.

Dvorsky was rejected by the mainstream Grail Movement, but the book managed to sell quite well, gaining him a modest number of followers who made contact with him by post. At the advice of a clairvoyant he trusted named

Josef Klimes (who also went by the name "Mr. Vidon"), Dvorsky and his wife Lucia established a compound in Northern Italy known as "The City," where the future heavenly kingdom would be centred. Klimes predicted massive global catastrophes presaging the end of the world and sending multitudes flocking to the safety of The City.

Some believers abandoned everything to make it to The City before the catastrophes hit. What they found there was a totalitarian microstate where Dvorsky's word was final. Purity tests were common, and many were expelled, particularly at the word of Klimes. The clairvoyant conducted psychic readings and declared that those with "bad auras" were to leave. Many of those expelled were extremely devout believers and were devastated at having been thrown out of the company of the righteous. Ten such former members reportedly attempted to starve themselves to death in the mountains surrounding The City in the hope of hastening their reincarnation into purer vessels.

Some members left of their own accord when the prophesied catastrophes did not materialize, but even then, Dvorsky continued to expel those who stayed behind until only his family remained. All told, about sixty individuals cycled through The City, though it never held more than fifteen at any one time. In 1995, Dvorsky and his wife were indicted for parental neglect for refusing to allow their children to attend school. The entire family went into hiding that summer and has not been heard from since.

Following this unfortunate affair, the Imanuelité were recognised as one of the most dangerous groups in the Czech Republic, and the mainstream Grail Movement had its reputation tarnished by Dvorsky's association with it. The involvement of members of Škrla's group in the Kuřim Case stood to be a public relations disaster of even greater scale. Artur Zatloukal, leader of the Movement in the Czech Republic, was quick to disavow Škrla and his followers, making it known that they had broken away eleven years earlier due to unspecified differences in doctrine.

A Clear Connection

Investigators still made the deduction that they could probably use what they knew about the mainstream Grail Movement to pattern Škrla's sect's behaviour. Believers in the Grail Message are known to cooperate fully with each other, and if the sect had been used as the medium through which the abuse was perpetrated, it was likely that other members besides those already implicated had been enlisted. Klára and Kateřina were being held separately but were almost conspiratorially silent about the involvement of anyone else. Investigators heavily suspected that there were a lot more people involved in the matter, and they were determined to root them all out.

To that effect, a series of raids was launched against members of Škrla's sect, searching for anything that could shed light on the motives that lay behind the abuse of Jakub and Ondrej as well as how Barbora's transformation into Ana was orchestrated. They managed to turn up something that could be of interest: dozens of medical documents, all of them for children and containing diagnoses for very serious illnesses, mostly leukaemia and various other cancers. The names were all of real children from the daycare centre Kateřina and Hana Bašova worked for (as had Barbora in the past), but the diagnoses were forged.

When medical experts looked over the documents, they came away with the impression that the forgeries had been based on a source written with professional medical knowledge, but contained technical errors, which indicated their contents had been filtered through a person who was not an oncologist with full, intimate knowledge of the correct terminology.

The investigators were willing to consider other hypotheses besides the documents having somehow been used in fabricating a paper trail for Ana. The most obvious one was that they had been used to make false insurance claims for the treatment of the illnesses, but some digging done in pursuit of that theory uncovered no evidence of insurance fraud being perpetrated using the documents. However, the documents did resemble those that had been provided to the investigators by Klára and Kateřina to "prove" Ana's background story and also contained similar errors. Evidence of their being of the same or similar provenance.

This all but confirmed the connection between the splinter sect and the fabrication of Ana, strengthening the case that there was indeed a connection with the abuse, as well. With the aid of social workers and the caregivers at the Brno Children's Institution, investigators slowly managed to coax more information out of Jakub and Ondrej. Both stated that two other male adults had been involved in abusing them. One of the adults was known to them as Jerome – a name that did not belong to anyone thus far regarded as a person of interest. If their knowing Hana Bašova as "Nenci" was any indication, it was likely that the name was a pseudonym. The investigators showed them images of splinter sect members and scored a hit: the boys identified the other two abusers as Jan Škrla and Jan Turek.

Jan Škrla was the son of Josef Škrla and brother to Barbora and studied geology at Brno's Masaryk University, while Turek was an entrepreneur and also ran a shelter rehabilitating aggressive dogs that would otherwise have to be euthanised. Apart from being members of the sect, both had a further connection with the other abusers and persons of interest: they had both worked part-time at Kateřina's daycare centre, and had both been members of the Ants scout club. Turek was arrested for causing grievous bodily harm on the 8th September 2008, mere days after his complicity was established. The younger Škrla and Hana Bašova, on the other hand, remained free for several months, as the boys' testimony was deemed insufficient to bring proceedings against them immediately.

The Horrifying Full Extent of the Abuse

Along with the revelation of the two further suspects, Jakub's and Ondrej's testimony finally revealed the horrific complete details of the abuse they had suffered at the hands of their mother and her accomplices.

The horror did not begin for Jakub and Ondrej until the summer of the previous year, 2006. Before then, Klára had shown no tendency towards abuse or violence whatsoever – it had all begun quite suddenly, and was immediately of such high intensity and brutality that the boys had been thrown into shock, unable to process what was happening to them. The boys had been taken by their mother and aunt, along with the person they knew as their sister Ana, to a cottage in the countryside in Veverská Bítýška. It was about half an hour's drive northwest of their home in Brno later to be joined by Hana Bašova, Jan Škrla, and Jan Turek. Rather than being a regular family holiday out in the great outdoors – of which they used to have many before Ana came into their lives – this one had a darker purpose.

Waiting for them at the cottage was a pair of dog cages into which they were stuffed, absolutely forbidden from communicating with each other. They had also been fed from dog bowls. Over a period of several days, they were only ever taken out of the cages to be subjected to the very worst of the cruel treatment they would experience. With bags over their heads, they were beaten with belt buckles and a bamboo pole, scratched with forks, had cigarettes stubbed out on their groins, and had hot water – hot enough to be agonising but not enough to cause permanent damage – slowly poured over their abdomens. On one occasion, Ondrej had his head held down in a bucket of water.

The torture was not only physical. It extended to the psychological, well beyond even the dehumanisation of being caged like dogs, their heads covered, they could not see who was doing what to them, but they could hear their jeers and taunts well enough. They were forced to memorize vulgar words and phrases, had industrial music blared at them in order to unsettle them, and were often forced to inflict harm on each other, as well. There was also a bizarre pantomime that can only be described as a ritual that was done to them. They were forced to dig shallow graves and lie in them, then being repeatedly told they were dead.

For some reason, Ondrej seems to have attracted the bulk of the torture. This singling out culminated in what was probably the most horrific and revolting act of the entire hideous experience. Ondrej was taken out of his cage and held down tightly to stop him escaping. Klára then cut a piece of flesh from his rear while he squirmed and screamed – the source of the circular indentation in his buttocks. While he still wept, the piece of meat was passed around and consumed by the adults present.

The abuse that followed when they returned from the cottage seems tame by comparison, but it was still far beyond what any child should ever experience. With stern admonishments not to mention what happened there or was happening at home, reinforced by extensive coaching on what to say should he ever be asked, Jakub returned to school after the summer.

The change in his demeanour did not go without notice, though – in the 2006-2007 school year, he missed a total of 214 hours of school, divided evenly over both halves of the year. He also missed out on every swimming practice and nature outing, as well as on a class trip to the Beskid mountains on the border with Poland – all probably to make sure he was never seen unclothed for anyone to ask unwelcome questions about the marks on his body.

Ondrej, on the other hand, was allowed to be home-schooled because of a diagnosis of a hearing problem, which was found to be completely nonexistent by Institution caregivers and social workers. He spent the rest of the year 2006 in the basement of the Beam daycare centre, chained to a desk and under the watchful eye of Hana Bašova, who occasionally beat him when she was aggravated. He was forced to urinate in a bucket, being released to defecate in the bathroom in the depths of the night. Jan Škrla occasionally brought him meals during this period, and he was periodically taken out for exercise by Jan Turek.

When Klára had secured the lease for the Kuřim house, he was transferred to his confinement in the under-stair closet, there to remain until his liberation -- thanks to Eduard Trdy's malfunctioning baby monitor.

Guessing at the Motives

The revelation of the full extent of what Jakub and Ondrej had experienced left the entire country stunned, sickened, and appalled. It also brought new life to the question everyone had been asking from the very beginning: *why*? Why had two innocent children been subjected to such a terrible ordeal by those they trusted the most?

Everything pointed to Josef Škrla's breakaway Grail Movement sect. There was no question it had provided the network of support necessary to inflict the abuse, and it was also likely that some factor of the doctrine followed by the sect had directly inspired the perpetrators' actions.

Overzealous Discipline?

Three possibilities presented themselves. The least sinister one was that the abuse was carried out with the intention of discipline – Klára and her co-accomplices had done it all for the purpose of training up the boys according to some twisted but still well intentioned (depending on one's perspective, of course) code of punishment for perceived wrongdoing or disobedience. This hypothesis assumed that Barbora Škrlová's story of simply trying to fit in with the way she felt inside was true, and had in fact been posited by Barbora herself during her brief resurfacing in Copenhagen.

The Grail Message's teaching on child-rearing advocates a firm and strong-handed approach to discipline if children are to grow to become righteous and upstanding adults, and it could be that Škrla's sect took this philosophy and amplified it to a monstrous degree. If Barbora's attestations that the boys had become excessively unruly were true (caused, perhaps, by her taking up so much of their mother's attention), Kateřina may have turned to the sect to help put them back on the right path.

Sexual Exploitation?

The second hypothesis came from evidence that had been collected from the house in Kuřim. From inside the under-stair cupboard itself, the camera that had been used to watch over Ondrej was found to have been of very high quality – recording in high definition at a time when such was a near a science fiction concept. It was impossible to find in electronics shops within the Czech Republic and had to have been imported at great cost.

Between the two of them, Klára and Kateřina rented three homes. Both had kept their original flats in Brno in addition to the house in Kuřim, which was rented in Kateřina's name – yet on paper did not seem capable of making nearly enough to maintain such large expenses. Klára had previously been a secretary in Brno but had been unemployed for a while before making the move to Kuřim, while Kateřina managed a daycare, neither of which are usually high-paying vocations. All of this raised a big question: where had the money come from?

The possible answer came from what the camera had been used for: like Eduard Trdý's set, Klára's was capable of recording. A videotape had been found in the house with three and a half hours of footage of Ondrej in the closet, tied by hand and foot to a shelf and, close to the end of it, falling asleep. In a sick irony, the footage was found recorded over a videotape of children's fairytales titled "Tales from Grandmother Sheep."

Added to Ondrej's automatic smiling reaction when being photographed by first responders, this points to the possibility that he was used to being photographed in this state and had been coached on how to present himself to the point it came to him naturally. This supported a theory that the torture was for the purpose of selling the images to sadomasochistic paedophiles.

A single video or collection of photographs of that kind of material could sell for hundreds of pounds at that time. The sale of a couple of dozen of each every month would go far towards supporting an extravagant lifestyle. Also possible was that the view of the closet was streamed live over the internet to select customers. There was also the possibility of more direct exploitation. The boys had largely been unable to see anyone when they were being tortured at the cottage, leaving open the possibility that some of their torturers had been paying "customers" who had coughed up large sums of money to directly satisfy their perverted desires.

Barbora's pantomime as Ana also factored into this theory. Her transformation was theorised as possibly having the same intent as repackaging a "product" for sick-minded individuals to better enjoy – if potential customers were under the impression that she was a thirteen-year-old girl, media featuring her would still fetch a good price. Her believably acting like a thirteen-year-old would also have worked well in fooling any customers who wished to perform acts on or with her in person. The big question here was whether Barbora had somehow been forced into this arrangement or been an active and willing participant.

Esoteric Transformation?

The third hypothesis posited a more esoteric explanation – that the abuse and certain other aspects surrounding it were more closely tied to the splinter sect's most deeply held beliefs. The details of this theory more directly resemble what we can immediately recognise as "cult activity": the commission of clandestine acts with the purpose of fulfilling some prophetic goal of the participants.

Barbora's transformation was a cornerstone of this theory. The Messianic origins of the Grail Movement were well known, and Jan Dvorsky's Imanuelite movement had proven its propensity for creating or inspiring offshoot revivals. It was seen as possible, then, that Barbora's transformation was initiated with the purpose of creating in her a new Messiah to deliver the faithful where previous ones had failed. Alternatively, the objective may have been less supernatural, that she was meant to be an icon or figurehead for the faithful to rally around.

Under this hypothesis, the attitude Jakub and Ondrej towards the person they knew as Ana provides a clue to the possible motivation for the abuse. Investigators had noticed how attached they were to her, but had initially thought it to be a simple familial bond that had formed since she had become a part of their lives. They had both been naturally friendly and gregarious children before the abuse, and it seemed natural that they would have accepted her into their lives.

The more they spoke about her, though, the more their adoration seemed too intense and their praise of her too glowing for simple sibling love. A caregiver at the institution recalled Jakub once saying that Ana was special, and when asked how, he said that she was chosen by God. When pressed for further details, Jakub clammed up and said he could not say any more. Their attitude towards Ana, it seemed, had been moulded by the adults in their lives according to some religious worldview.

Every other relationship the boys had seemed manipulated as to make them more aloof. This was observed in their relationship with each other. Before the abuse, they had been as fond of each other as two young siblings separated in age by only a couple of years could be, but that close brotherly bond had been eroded to the point that they barely acknowledged each other at all and often displayed outright hostility towards one another.

Being cut off from their father and extended family created a gulf between them and the boys. They had lost friends – Ondrej had, of course, had no opportunities to make friends while he was in captivity, while Jakub had been heavily discouraged from interacting with his classmates while at school. Team sports, social outings, and other activities had been stopped, leaving them no opportunities to socialize with children of their own age.

Klára herself was not spared – in the months following the visit to the cottage, she had been isolated from the boys while Jakub was watched over by his aunt Kateřina, and Ondrej had been held captive at the daycare centre under the unsympathetic eye of Hana Bašova.

The only person with whom the boys had a positive relationship was Barbora, in the form of Ana. The physical abuse they suffered also often centred around Ana: in the middle of nearly every night they would be woken up and told that she was going to receive two lashes across the back – and she would only be spared if they each took one for themselves. They would comply almost without fail.

These details of the boys' relationships seemed just as purposeful as the sudden initiation of the abuse itself, and it led to the crux of this theory. If Barbora was to be some idol or icon, then perhaps the boys were destined to be her protectors, and the abuse had been perpetrated with the objective of reinforcing their loyalty to her while purging all others. The boys' behaviour following their ordeal hinted at an end-goal of creating a pair of unthinking, unfeeling, utterly loyal and dedicated guardians fit to stand at the side of whatever Barbora was destined to be.

The breaking down a person's will until they will unquestioningly accept authority and act without any personal motivation or thought of self has been in practice for centuries. When the practice gained its modern name, the "newspeak" word *brainwashing,* as coined by the totalitarian Big Brother's brutal one-party regime in George Orwell's classic novel *1984,* the use of physical and psychological trauma was a central pillar of the act. Its efficacy in achieving its central goal while preserving the victim's functionality has never been proven, but that has never stopped real-world aspiring totalitarians and crackpot movements from trying. By directing their effort onto the more pliable minds of a pair of young children, the splinter sect may have believed they would succeed.

The child pornography and cult theories soon took prominence in people's minds. Everything pointed toward a clear objective behind the entire affair – simple undirected frustration or random hysteria on Kateřina and her accomplices' parts were not enough to explain it. The police, more grounded in temporal affairs, as they tend to be, leaned towards the child pornography theory but did not discount the possibility of a religious explanation.

Chapter 3 – The Journey of a Thousand Miles

The final third of the year 2007 saw a great deal of searching for further clues in the case, but with no major breakthroughs. The suspects already in custody were keeping their lips tightly sealed, with the exception of occasional statements professing either no wrongdoing or, on Klára's part, an attestation of the purity of her intentions and regret over what happened, but without giving away any details for what had prompted it all.

It seemed there would be no extracting information from the suspects until it could be prised out of them at trial. Eager as investigators were to get to that stage, there was still a massive loose end waving in the breeze, and as long as it was left untied the case could not be considered complete enough to be closed.

Barbora Škrlová had neither been seen nor heard from since dropping off the radar a second time back in August. With the part she had played in the entire affair as unclear as it was, proceeding with the trial without her would leave far too many questions unanswered. At the very least, she had to answer for the deception she had pulled, and at worst she was an accomplice to, if not an instigator of, the abuse the boys had suffered. She had to be found, and her version of events had to be heard and thoroughly scrutinised in order to ascertain the complete truth. As a result, prosecutors held off on commencing the trial while the investigators worked to locate Barbora.

Barbora had last been seen in Denmark. It was also known that she had passed through Germany on her way there, and there was a possibility that she had at some recent point in time been in Sweden as well. The investigators' foreign inquiries concentrated on these three nations. Their patience in waiting before proceeding with the trial paid off shortly after the turn of the year, but true to her previous fashion, when Barbora finally resurfaced it was in a completely unexpected place – and the way she had evaded detection was a deception even more audacious and astounding than her masquerade as Ana.

At the heart of winter

Situated at a latitude of about 69° north, 190 miles above the Arctic Circle (which encircles the top of the world at approximately 66°), the city of Tromsø is recognised as the northernmost city in the world. It is in the land of the midnight sun and midday darkness – between the middle of May and the end of July, the sun does not set in Tromsø, and between the end of November and the middle of January, it never rises.

A troubled boy

On the 5th of January 2008, during the long night of the depth of winter, a man walked into a car rental office to drop off a vehicle he had hired several weeks before in Oslo. As he was processing the paperwork for returning the car, police burst in with guns drawn, ordered him to lie on the floor, and cuffed him. The man was named Michal Riha, and the reason for his arrest was his travelling companion: a thirteen-year-old boy who had been whisked away – apparently abducted – from an orphanage in Oslo several weeks previously.

The boy was called Adam, and he was ostensibly the son of a Czech playwright named Martin Fahrner. Fahrner had immigrated to Norway from the Czech Republic at the end of the previous summer with his family and had been working for the Nordic Black Theatre, an avant-garde theatre company in Oslo. While Fahrner's wife and their other children returned to the Czech Republic in September, Adam had begun attending a school in Oslo.

By appearances, Adam seemed like a normal thirteen-year-old boy, sporting the disaffected expression common to adolescents and quite fond of skateboarding.

His teachers noticed a few odd things about him, though: he looked older than his years – some estimated he looked sixteen at the least, and he was very thin and his head shaven, with seemingly permanent dark circles around his eyes, leading them to wonder whether he suffered from cancer or some other serious illness. During his enrolment, he had been placed into a year-long intensive Norwegian language class due to his being a fresh immigrant to the country, but as he interacted with teachers and classmates, it became obvious that his grasp of the language was actually quite good.

They also noticed some in some of his behaviours, signs that he bore some kind of mental scarring, possibly from past trauma. He seemed nervous a lot of the time and afraid of loud noises: once, when a teacher entered a classroom, banged the door shut, and made a loud and boisterous greeting to the class, Adam had suffered a hysterical breakdown.

The possible source of the trauma was revealed in the extremely disturbing stories he told: stories of being abused by his father and rented out to older men for sexual purposes. His stories were very specific, describing in detail the acts that were performed on him. Teachers were obviously concerned and had to determine if the stories were true. They brought in a psychologist to assess and counsel him.

Adam also had to be removed from his father's custody and the man locked up if he had performed any of the acts described. It took a while for the psychologist to coax enough information out of Adam to call in the authorities. The final straw was a drawing he made of seven children with blood on their hands and feet and a man standing over and verbally threatening them. Adam himself had been child number seven, he said, and he and the six other children had all been tortured and abused together. Finally, in early December, Fahrner was arrested on suspicion of child abuse and Adam placed in an orphanage.

On the 16th of December, a few days after Adam was separated from his erstwhile abuser, the orphanage organised an outing for the children in its care. While on the outing, Adam suddenly dashed off into a car that was idling nearby, which then sped off.

Voluntary as the escape seemed, it was immediately assumed that Adam had been abducted by child traffickers, probably accomplices of whichever ring Fahrner had been renting him out to. A nationwide manhunt commenced. Adam's face was plastered all over the nation's TV stations and newspapers, along with pleas to report any sightings to the police.

The hunt for Adam

The next time Adam was seen was on the 19th of the month in Bergen, just under 300 miles west of Oslo. He was in the company of a man – likely Michal Riha – and was holding the man's hand as a son would with his father's. Together, they had entered the Neptun hotel in Bergen requesting to use the phone. The receptionist who attended to them was named Natalia Stormark, and she by chance happened to be one of the few people who knew nothing about the missing Adam. She later explained that she never read newspapers or watched the news. She still found their request odd: they had a mobile phone with them, so why would they need to use the hotel telephone?

By their accents, she guessed that they were Russian and suspected they may have been attempting a con: in the lobby of the hotel were several valuable paintings, and she suspected they were attempting to steal them. After they left without incident, she called the police with their descriptions just in case they were what she suspected. The hotel received a return call the next day, asking probing questions about the pair's appearance. When asked whether the boy seemed afraid or under duress, Stormark had replied that he seemed reasonably untroubled. *"Vypadali jako otec se synem"* ["They looked like father

54

and son"], she said. Man and boy had been holding hands - *"To u nás v Norsku třináctiletí kluci normálně nedělají"* ["Here in Norway you wouldn`t find a 13-year-old boy doing that"].

Fahrner and his family had not come to Norway alone: they had travelled into the country together with Michal Riha and his sister. When police attempted to trace their whereabouts, they discovered that he had taken several weeks off sick from his job at a computer store in Oslo and had hired a car earlier on the very day of Adam's disappearance. From this information, they deduced that Riha was likely the person who had spirited Adam away.

Finding the car on the road would be easier said than done, particularly since Riha's intentions and final destination were not known. It was probable that he would eventually have to return the car to another branch of the hire company, though, and employees were alerted to be on the lookout for him. This strategy eventually paid off when Riha and Adam finally walked into the branch in Tromsø – 1020 miles as the crow flies away from their starting point in Oslo, twenty days after setting out.

The rental dealership's employees immediately called in the police, and Riha was arrested. Adam was finally rescued, but he had a surprise for the police – "he" was not a thirteen-year-old boy. Rather, she was a woman and she was thirty-three years old, and her name was Barbora Škrlová.

Shock and betrayal

If those who had briefly interacted with Ana Mauerová in the Czech Republic had been stunned by the revelation of her true identity, those who had spent time with Adam felt an order of magnitude worse upon receiving the news. Not only had they spent months in his company, but they had also believed and come to empathise with the supposed horror he had gone through. Discovering that it had all been a ruse – and possibly one perpetrated with the intent of

55

covering up real child abuse – was distressing enough for some of them to need counselling.

In a press interview with a Czech outlet, Ingjerd Eriksen, headmistress of the school "Adam" had attended in Oslo, could not reconcile in her mind the truth that had been revealed with the boy who had been in her presence just weeks earlier. "Let's call him Adam instead," she said when she was asked about Barbora. "For me, it's Adam."

It had been Fahrner's wife, Helena, who had brought "Adam" to the school for enrolment. When asked if she had been shown any documentary evidence of Adam's identity, Eriksen recalled that she had been told that he did not have a passport. Helena had instead shown her own passport, in which Adam was listed as a dependant.

The couple actually did have a biological son named Adam – he returned to the Czech Republic along with the rest of his family while Barbora remained hiding behind his identity. Helena had also requested that the "Adam" she had brought to the school be excused from gym classes, and as a result Barbora never had to change clothes in the presence of anyone while at school.

Homecoming

Her true identity revealed, Barbora was arrested along with Riha. Unlike when she had turned up in Denmark, this time she had an outstanding arrest warrant for the two complaints made against her by the Institution and Masaryk University in Brno. She was extradited to the Czech Republic and on the 9th of January landed in Prague, finally stepping once again onto home soil wearing a bulky overcoat and tight-fitting skullcap, tightly clutching a teddy bear.

Even though he had known the truth about Barbora's identity and that the stories that had led to his arrest were untrue, Martin Fahrner had avoided spilling the beans about her. Once the truth came out, however, the charge for which he had been arrested was dropped. Unfortunately, his life in Norway was done – he had lost his job upon his arrest, and the truth, when it came out, was still too unpalatable for him to ever be employable there again.

With his family under intense scrutiny, his wife had been forced to withdraw their three children from school to protect them from the media frenzy. Fahrner returned to the Czech Republic so that he could be with them. Shortly after his return, Fahrner gave a short interview to the press. It did not explain much or shed much light on anything. Except for an assertion that he had not had anything to do with her initial escape from the Institution, he would not answer as to when Barbora had come into his company. Neither would he tell exactly why she had taken on his son's identity.

There were many complicated parallel stories to be told that no one would understand, he said, but she had seemed afraid of something all along – what it was he could not say. When asked whether he was a member of a cult, Fahrner replied with derision. The movement to which he belonged was a recognised religion in several countries. An accusation that someone was part of a cult was a sure way of rousing fear in the Czech Republic – as well as reaping a harvest of television ratings, website hits, and newspaper sales.

Another interview that hit the papers after Barbora's arrest was that of Josef Kolinsky, Barbora's former spokesperson during the brief time she had raised her head above the sand in Denmark, who had recently resurfaced himself. He had first met with Barbora in Sweden, he said, together with her father Josef – along with Martin and Helena Fahrner, who had been introduced as family friends. This places Fahrner's interaction with Barbora soon after she escaped the Czech Republic.

During his interrogation and shortly after being arrested, Barbora's brother Jan stated that he had seen a picture of Barbora in another disguise and carrying an assault rifle, and he claimed to have been told she was an agent working for Russia. When asked about this, Kolinsky said it was a fabrication, part of a story Josef Škrla had hatched to throw the investigation off Barbora's trail. When he was presented with this plan, Kolinsky said, he had refused to be a part of it and advised going to the authorities as a wiser course of action.

On the whole, Kolinsky's involvement with Škrla and his cadre had left a sour taste in his mouth. In meeting several other members of the splinter sect, his policeman's intuition had left him with a not-too-reassuring impression of just what they were capable of. Asked if he thought it credible that Jan Škrla had participated in the sexual abuse of his own sister, as some had speculated, Kolinsky did not completely discount the possibility. He also could not say with absolute certainty that the sect was not involved in the abuse or that, if they were involved, there were no other children besides Jakub and Ondrej being abused.

New allegations

Upon landing in the Czech Republic, Barbora was immediately handed over to the custody of the Brno police and transported there. Richard Novak, a lawyer who had been representing Jan Škrla, took Barbora on as well. Novak attempted to have her immediately released on bail, but the request was denied due to the high flight risk she posed – prosecutors had learned their lesson worked to make sure another disappearance would be impossible. Whether she had participated in the abuse of Jakub and Ondrej was also still unanswered, and with that more serious charge potentially hanging over her head, they could take no chances.

Following her unveiling and arrest, Barbora appeared to be in a poor mental state and so could not immediately face interrogation. She was placed in a special "crisis cell," separate from potential attacks by other prisoners – partly to avoid over-stimulating her and causing further disorientation, but also to protect her from other prisoners. Among the hierarchy of inmates in any corrections system in the world, those who harm children are invariably loathed and seen as the lowest of offenders. The fact that Barbora was not even a suspect in Jakub and Ondrej's abuse at that point might not have prevented some overzealous individuals from harassing her all the same – it was better to be safe than sorry.

Barbora's psychological state stabilised over the next few days. Finally, on the fifteenth of the month, she was deemed sufficiently stable to answer investigators' questions and went through an hour-and-a-half-long preliminary session. Gone was the infantile manner of speech and action she had exhibited in Copenhagen – aside from an apparent timidity that showed itself in her body language and the softness of her voice, she spoke normally.

The first interview went smoothly, with Barbora cooperating fully. She claimed to have been a victim of torture herself, and that her torturers had filmed and photographed her. A physical examination had shown possible evidence supporting this – there were scars from cuts and bruises that may have come from burns on her body. Some of the wounds did not at first examination seem to have been self-inflicted or to be the result of masochism, while others seemed more ambiguous. They would need to be scrutinised further to determine their origin.

Shortly after this revelation, Richard Novak resigned from representing Jan Škrla and began to represent Barbora alone. Representing them both now presented a conflict of interest – Barbora's allegation placed her and her brother on opposing sides of the coming legal battle -- whether she too would stand accused of abusing the boys along with him and the rest of the defendants or not. From that point on, Škrla was represented by Zdenek Jaros, a public defender.

Barbora's subsequent interviews were a lot less successful, though. She became uncooperative, answering questions in a general sense and refusing to be drawn into divulging any specific details. Frustration with her mounted, and the courts ordered a two-month long psychiatric evaluation. Richard Novak attempted once again to have her released, stating that continuing to hold her would only be justified if she had evaded arrest out of her own volition. While in Copenhagen, she had not been a wanted person. Hence, her going back into hiding (which was prompted by fear of reprisals if she was forcefully returned to the Czech Republic) did not provide sufficient grounds to keep her imprisoned. After that, she had acted wholly at the mercy of other people, and when she had finally had the opportunity to come clean, she volunteered her identity to the Norwegian police out of her own choice and without duress. All the same, the courts once again turned down the appeal.

Klára speaks

Since the very beginning of the case, Klára had held onto the belief that Ana had been real. Even when Barbora resurfaced in Copenhagen, she still could not be sure the confession of impersonating her thirteen-year-old adoptive daughter was genuine. The only evidence the public had of Barbora's presence there had been news reports, none of which had featured any photographs or footage taken of her.

Once Barbora had been arrested, though, the evidence was plain to see: she reiterated her confession of impersonating Ana even as she protested her own victimhood, and photographs of her as Adam proved her perfectly capable of getting away with that sort of deception. With this realisation, Klára's reticence to cooperate with the investigation finally broke. "Ana" had participated in some of the abuse, she revealed – during the trip to the cottage in the countryside, Kateřina had instructed Ana-Barbora to forcefully hold Ondrej's head under water, and she had complied. She and Jakub had also on a few occasions been instructed to beat Ondrej.

Armed with this testimony, prosecutors had what they needed to move against Barbora, and on the 11th February 2008, she was charged with child abuse for the part she had played. Rolled into that charge would be the consideration of her not having intervened or contacted the authorities. If she were found to have had diminished responsibility for the more serious charge due to psychological reasons, the same would apply to the less serious one, whereas if she were found to have acted with competency all along, a single sentence would cover both.

As soon as she was charged, Barbora's tune changed: she was once again willing to divulge all she could to the police. Over a series of interviews with both the police and the press, she revealed her version of events.

Her new testimony differed significantly from the one she had presented in Copenhagen. She had not willingly undergone the transformation into Ana, she said, and Kateřina had not been a benevolent helper who had assisted her to assume an outward form that reflected her inner identity. Through a combination of physical and psychological abuse, coupled with a regimen of drugs, she had been forced into it by the Mauerová sisters.

The ringleader in the effort had been Hana Bašova. A few years before the formal adoption, Bašova had confronted her, saying she had a "bad attitude" that needed to be gotten rid of. Barbora apparently suffered from epilepsy as well as a host of psychological problems and was at the time almost wholly dependent on Kateřina. As a result, she was unable to prevent what followed.

Over the next few years, she had been forced to take a potent cocktail of psychotropics – she recalled injections and being forced to ingest pills and plant material – which rendered her mind and entire sense of self a malleable clay to

61

be formed into whatever her abusers wished. Consequently, the entire experience was a blur in her memory, and she could only remember hazy patches of it.

As Ondrej later did, she claimed that she had been locked up in the basement at the daycare centre she had worked for. Her captors had begun by training her to take on different names and identities, she claimed, being drilled on each persona for hours and receiving a beating if she slipped up at any point. Her will had been worn down steadily until she did not know who she was anymore, and once that point had passed, the persona of Ana was built up to take Barbora's place.

Barbora said that before "Ana's" formal adoption by Kateřina, she had been allowed to contact and occasionally visit her mother. She was instructed to "be Barbora" during those visits, even when her personality had been subsumed to the point that she felt like Ana all the time. If she failed to stick to her instructions, she was warned, there would be dire consequences for both her and her mother. The amount of time she spent in her mother's presence had to be kept as short as possible, as a long visit would increase the chances of her slipping up or her mother noticing that something was wrong. A mobile phone call from Bašova or Kateřina was both her signal and excuse that it was time to leave.

Barbora alleged that the adoption of "Ana" by Klára and the commencement of the abuse of Jakub and Ondrej was simply the continuation of what had been happening to her for years. All three of them had been forced to inflict pain on each other – she admitted to drowning Ondrej, but if she had refused it would have been her head going under the water. Disobedience was never an option – refusing to perform an act would mean that it was inflicted on her to an even harsher extent.

The purpose of it all had been, in Barbora's words, to sell her to "evil men who do ugly things to children," affirming one of the early hypotheses. Many times she had been tortured, while blindfolded, at the hands of males whose voices she did not recognise. She remembered one name, though – a man named Hansen had been allowed a special privilege, perhaps one he had paid a very high price for: while she was tied and bent over a table, Hansen had slit her clothes and raped her.

After Ondrej was discovered in the closet, Barbora had to make sure no one had the opportunity to examine her body lest her true age be discovered. She had been helped to escape the Institution by two men she could not name who helped her out of the window, took her into the woods, and transported her to Denmark. She had been allowed to meet her father there before being whisked away to Norway, where Martin Fahrner had forced her to take on his son Adam's identity. The escape had provided her no respite, she claimed – she was still forced to service "customers" while in Scandinavia. Finally, she said her captors had been apprehended by the police, and she had gratefully revealed her true identity to them as her saviours.

Chapter 4 – The trial

Barbora's alternate account added another complex element to the case. The only way to untangle it all would be to go to trial, and with her present and apparently willing to cooperate, it could finally begin. On the 2nd April, 2008, over eleven months after it had begun, the police officially closed the investigation. All told, the case file – composed of testimony, collected evidence, and expert analysis – contained six thousand pages of documents.

Tying all the knots

Even with the closing of the case, there was still a lot of preliminary trial work to be done. Officials had to be assigned to the trial and a few other details had to be ironed out.

A judge was assigned to the case through a lottery system. There are sixteen judges who preside over the Brno Municipal Court. Each of them is assigned a number, and cases are assigned to each judge in ascending order according to their availability.

Assigning the judge

The judge assigned to the case at first was Martin Vrbik. Vrbik was forced to resign from the case, however. He had been friends with the sister of the two accused, Gabriela Mauerová, a decade and a half earlier, and was familiar with the rest of the family. Tenuous as their connection was, this constituted a conflict of interest. He voluntarily disclosed his connection and stepped down from the case. Such conflicts are not that rare in Brno – they tend to occur once or twice a month from judges being assigned to the cases of their own relatives or acquaintances, current and former.

The case was then passed to the next judge in line, Pavel Göth, who fortunately had no connection with any of the accused.

On the 21st April, the accused were formally indicted. The Mauerová sisters, Hana Bašova and Jan Škrla, faced up to twelve years' imprisonment for deprivation of liberty of minors and the abuse of persons entrusted to their care, while Barbora Škrlová and Jan Turek faced up to eight years for aggravated cruelty.

The statement from the Regional Prosecutor's Office in Brno that accompanied the indictments cited the abuse Jakub and Ondrej had suffered: the beatings, physical and psychological torture, humiliation, and extended durations of imprisonment in dark rooms. It also mentioned the practical effect that the abuse seemed designed to produce: severing the children's bonds of family and creating beings with no will of their own, desensitized to violence and pain.

A matter of reputation

Kateřina and Barbora were also indicted for malicious damage to the reputation of the Brno Children's Institution for the way the Ana deception had tarnished its name. The Institution had weathered a considerable share of the media storm following Ana's escape and suffered public reprimand for it. Curious sightseers were sometimes seen lurking around their premises, and the words "Kauza Kuřim" were at one point spray-painted onto one of their buildings by a vandal.

In a short hearing before the main trial, both Barbora and Kateřina were acquitted of this charge. The reasoning behind the decision was that the deception had begun long before Barbora-as-Ana came into contact with the Institution, and it had not been undertaken with the express objective of bringing the Institution into disrepute. Besides, the Institution had to take its own share of the blame: they should have done an immediate medical exam on "Ana" as soon as she arrived in their care. Doing so would have uncovered the deception without the Institution losing face. It would also have prevented the significant cost and delay that had come with the search for Barbora. The media attention they had received was not admissible as detrimental – they would have to live with it the same as any other organisation that catches the media's eye.

Requests and objections

The court also had to address outstanding issues brought up by the accused. Klára's attorney Daniel Sevcik requested that the trial be held "in camera," meaning that all hearings be held in private without any access for the public or the press. Sevcik stated that the involvement of minors in the case made it very sensitive – the boys had already faced a great deal of media attention, and having the trial itself endlessly covered would not serve their best interests. The other defence attorneys *and* the prosecution back the request. If it went through, details of the trial would not be available to the public in real time. Instead, they would be released in monthly updates heavily edited by the court.

Kateřina's attorney, Pavel Holub, objected to one of the experts who would be testifying in the trial. Marta Skulova was a psychiatrist who had assessed Jakub and Ondrej shortly after they were liberated. Holub alleged that she was biased: Skulova was a financial contributor to the Brno Children's Institution and so could not be relied upon to have been impartial in her assessment.

The objection failed to stand: Skulova had made a donation of 5,000 Koruna in December 2007, long after she had assessed the boys and made her report. The gift had been part of her usual round of Christmas donations, and she had made it simply because she had become familiar with the Institution through her work with the boys.

One small final matter...

The preliminary findings of the psychiatric assessment of Barbora Škrlová were finally announced. They would have bearing on whether Barbora would be declared fit to stand trial. If her story of having been forced into taking on the identity of Ana and being a victim of extreme mental torture herself was found to be true, she could be spared before the trial even began due to diminished responsibility. The assessment had found her to be mentally fit and healthy enough to be held culpable, and that she had acted completely of her own volition. The finer details would be revealed later on during the trial, but the short statement that was released asserted that Barbora had wilfully manipulated Klára, and that she suffered from a personality disorder that did not constitute grounds to block her prosecution.

With the question of Barbora's fitness to face prosecution answered, the trial was ready to begin.

On the 17th June 2008, the Kuřim Case trial opened amid another media storm. Despite both the prosecution and defence reiterating their request for the trial to be closed to the public, Judge Pavel Göth declined the request, stating that the case as a whole did not meet the necessary criteria of sensitivity. In certain extraordinary cases, though – such as the unpleasant but necessary viewing of the recordings of Ondrej – the public would be excluded.

As a result, the press came out in force – over three dozen journalists were present, including a few from Norwegian outlets. The hearing had not even officially begun when they received their first morsel. As she was passing in front of the press box, Renata Škrlová, mother to Barbora and Jan Škrla, burst out, *"Obžaloba je výsledkem bezbřehé tuposti policie. Má dcera je nevinná"* ["The indictment is a result of the endless ignorance of the police. My daughter is innocent"].

Events according to Klára Mauerová's testimony

Klára was the first person to give her testimony in the trial. It was evident from the moment she entered the courtroom for the first hearing that she was barely holding herself together. She had shuffled in dejectedly, her head bowed and eyes red from crying, and as the charges were read, she began to weep and continued to do so through her testimony. Her voice barely rising above a mournful whisper, she began by confirming the validity of the charges laid against her, calling her part in the abuse of her own children as a terrible thing, but explaining that she had done it all with the purest of intentions.

A child in need

It had all begun in the summer of 2003, Klára said, when Kateřina had asked her about her interest in social childcare and exactly why she wanted to study it. It was so that she could help children, she had replied, especially abused and orphaned children. At the time, Klára had thought the query innocuous enough, but as she thought about it in hindsight, this was probably when Kateřina had found her way in.

Later that year, sometime in autumn, Kateřina invited Klára to her apartment. There she showed Klára a child's bed with children's toys on it and confided a secret to her: she had taken in a child from Norway at the behest of a secret organisation. The girl had been rescued from human traffickers and had suffered horrendous sexual abuse throughout her childhood, she was told – and was also dying of leukaemia. Because the traffickers were still seeking the girl, Kateřina entreated Klára to absolute secrecy and asked if she could perform a test for bone marrow compatibility with the girl, who needed a transplant.

Once Klára had given her word of confidentiality, she was allowed to meet the girl. The child was introduced as Vatase, and she certainly looked ill and slender to the point of emaciation. Her mannerisms were also very unusual, avoiding eye contact and speaking very haltingly in a low voice.

Klára said that she had never made the connection between the child before her and Barbora Škrlová. Kateřina had told her that Barbora had passed away some time before, and the difference in appearance and mannerisms was so total and drastic that the possibility of impersonation had never even flitted through her mind. Her only direct interaction with Barbora before then had been during one camp with the Mravenci several years earlier, and the woman she remembered had been plump and had a completely different voice and physical demeanour.

She also seemed disoriented and often slipped between speaking Czech and Norwegian. Kateřina explained that the trauma she had experienced over the years, coupled with her frail physical condition, had left her with severe mental scars and cognitive issues. She reacted to most people with fear – too many had hurt her throughout her short life and her sense of trust had been obliterated, if it had ever had the chance to flourish at all.

As they spent time in each other's company, Kateřina commented on how the child appeared to have a different reaction towards Klára – she seemed drawn towards her and was being more open than she had ever been with a new person. She had even confided in Klára: her real name was Ana. Kateřina seemed surprised by this, as Ana never told anyone her real name.

The results of the bone marrow compatibility test returned as negative. Klára could not donate for Ana, but there was still a way she could help – the way that Ana had taken an immediate liking for her was remarkable. Ana's existence until then had been a blur of pain and fear, but the rest of her life need not be the same now that she was free of her abusers. The time she had left was short – she wouldn't live beyond the age of sixteen. She deserved for the rest of it to be as comfortable as possible, and if she could be around someone she trusted, her quality of life would be vastly improved.

Kateřina asked if Klára could take Ana into her home and provide the stability and love that she needed. Klára was hesitant – another child would be a huge responsibility – as Jakub and Ondrej had taught her already – let alone one with the needs and challenges Ana had. Kateřina had then enlisted the help of a doctor who was one of her contacts in the organisation that had brought Ana into her care.

The doctor became one of the most influential figures in Klára's life – it was his advice that initiated and encouraged what would later happen to Jakub and Ondrej, and yet she never met him or even knew his name. It is likely that he was a fabrication – the only communication Klára ever received from him was through text messages and the occasional phone call, but the mobile phone number the communiqués were received through was traced to Kateřina's ownership. So trusting had Klára been of her elder sister that Kateřina's word had been all she needed to trust the doctor's counsel.

The doctor spoke to Klára over the phone and reiterated that she was the best person to help Ana live the rest of her life in comfort and security. Klára's objections slowly dissolved as the values she had been taught by her parents asserted themselves and she began to see helping Ana as her God-given duty.

When Ana moved in with the family in December 2005, she at first reacted to Jakub and Ondrej with her characteristic apprehension but warmed up to them over time. The relationship of all three of them with each other was normal and healthy at that time – it wasn't until the cottage in the woods that the nefarious manipulation took place.

An overwhelming task

Taking care of Ana proved even more difficult than Klára had expected. Her health issues required a great deal of attention and regular treatment – she suffered from seizures, for which she would need restraint. Klára was also told that Ana had hydrocephaly and needed daily spinal massage from the base of her skull down her backbone – sometimes for up to eight hours a night. She was also encouraged to stroke Ana's genital area during these massages – in order to "comfort" her and help them "bond" as mother and daughter.

Ana was also extremely emotionally demanding, directly clamouring for Klára's attention. She demanded gifts and treats regularly, and would throw explosive tantrums when she did not get her way. She sometimes behaved very dangerously, once threatening to jump out of the window of their apartment while holding a knife, and Klára had to be on guard with her at train stations, as she always seemed to be on the verge of jumping out onto the tracks. Klára did what she could to placate her outbursts and keep her as happy as possible.

Trying to balance this new home life with her studies was a monumental task for Klára, and she often went on as little as three hours of sleep in a day. The stress began to wear her down and, to make matters worse, Jakub and Ondrej began acting out, probably in an attempt to regain the maternal attention they had lost to Ana. The stress probably acted to exaggerate the boys' behavioural problems in Klára's mind, and she also had Kateřina (and her secret organisation) whispering in her ear and convincing her that it was a far worse problem than it really was.

A solution proposed

The mysterious doctor was waiting in the wings to offer Klára a solution for the boys' behaviour: what they needed was a serious attitude adjustment. If they continued on the path they were on, she was told, their bad behaviour would continue into adulthood and they would end up in prison. A taste of the horror of prison life would give them a glimpse into their own destiny, which would swiftly set them back on the correct path.

The weekend at the cottage in Veverska Bityska was thus planned. Klára claimed that she had not participated in any of the planning – all of that had been done by Kateřina, supposedly according to the doctor's instructions, and with the help of Hana Bašova, Jan Turek (who provided the dog cages the boys were forced to sleep in) and Jan Škrla. When the abuse commenced at the cottage and continued after that, Klára acted wholly as instructed by Kateřina. She was told to participate and inflict her own share of pain on them – all the while, she said, with no other intention in her heart but to correct the crooked path she perceived her natural children to be following. As her children lay whimpering in their separate dog cages in shock after the first harsh ministrations, she was forbidden by Turek and Škrla to help or comfort them.

Klára asserted that, to the best of her knowledge, torture pornography of her children had never been disseminated nor been an objective at any point, though she did not speculate on what the actual reasons were. She also claimed never to have at any point in her life been involved in the Škrla sect's activities. The only exposure she had ever had to the Grail Movement's teachings was a book Kateřina had given her several years earlier, but she had never been interested in it and had never attended any ceremonies. The only religious motivation she claimed ever to have had had been to help Ana and raise her children well.

The adoption

Another issue that the trial shed a light on was the adoption of Ana. In her testimony, Klára explained the substitution of Viktor Skala's daughter Maria for the court hearings and DNA tests mandated by the process. The deception had been explained to her as necessary to minimize the possibility of Ana's supposed abusers discovering her whereabouts.

In their respective testimonies, Viktor Skala and his wife Zuzana claimed never to have known that their daughter was used to commit perjury. Zuzana had worked at the Paprska daycare centre with Kateřina, Barbora and Hana Bašova. She admitted to both she and her husband being members of Škrla's breakaway sect from the Grail Movement. She maintained, however, that neither of them had privileged positions within its structure and were not party to any secret activities it might have been undertaking. Maria herself was a child, and all she had needed to be told to secure her compliance was that it was all a game.

Maria Skalova was very different from Ana in both appearance and mannerisms. Kateřina and Bašova had worked on her to make her a believable facsimile: her hair was dyed several shades darker, and she wore brown contact lenses to cover the natural blue of her eyes. She had been instructed to observe Ana's mannerisms and reproduce them as closely as possible to create the illusion that she was autistic.

At the supposed instruction of the doctor, Kateřina had concocted the story of Ana having previously been in the custody of her and Klára's grandmother. The two of them had then approached their mother Eliška and told her Ana's story and why they needed to pull the wool over the authorities' eyes. Out of sympathy, Eliška had agreed to perjure herself if it meant helping her daughters give an unfortunate child a safe home.

Turek testifies

Klára was the only one of the defendants to fully admit her guilt. The first of the others to offer a detailed rebuttal was Jan Turek, who maintained that he had neither known about nor directly participated in the abuse of Jakub and Ondrej. The allegations brought against him had destroyed his reputation and completely killed the business of his clothing salon.

His only connection to the case, he said, was the provision of the dog cages. Kateřina, who knew about his work with canines, had approached him asking if he could help her borrow a couple. The cages he had procured for her were not even his – he had borrowed them himself from the Brno police, with whom he had been working at the time. If he had known what the cages would be used for, he said, he would never have helped Kateřina get hold of them.

Turek also claimed never to have been involved with the Grail Movement or the splinter sect. He had been on friendly terms with Josef Škrla during his time with the scout troop, but said he had never been drawn into any esoteric beliefs. He also stated that he had barely known Barbora, and that he had never been close enough to Kateřina to know about Ana at all, let alone the fact that she was Barbora in disguise.

Stories from the past

Turek maintained that he was incapable of harming another human being, but his past suggested otherwise – he was divorced, and his marriage had been rife with accusations of his being physically, verbally, and emotionally abusive. His ex-wife Lucia, with whom he shared a son, had called the police several times during their marriage, and she had spent five months living in a shelter for battered women.

Since his past behaviour offered a clue to his character, one of the witnesses called up by the court was Lucia Turkova herself. Her prepared statement was surprising – she called him a devoted husband and father, as well as a great teacher who was often approached for advice by other parents and mentioned nothing about the abuse she had previously claimed. When she was asked about it, she surprised the court even further: it was *she* who had initiated any physical attacks. Whenever she did so, Turek had never responded in kind. Instead, she said, he would leave the house with a beer in his hand and a dog on a leash and take a walk to cool off. When he failed to retaliate, she would inflict injuries on herself in order to make her allegations that he was an abuser more believable.

Turek listened to this testimony with his face buried in his hands. When Lucia stepped down from the stand, he thanked her for her supposed truthfulness, and for having the courage to express details that painted her in a bad light that he had kept private.

Lucia's testimony painted Turek in an almost saintly light, and his girlfriend at the time of the trial had nothing bad to say about him. Turek had been in a relationship with Marketa Stejskalova since 2006, and she stated that he had never shown either her or her twin sons from a previous marriage any aggression. Stejskalova had also suffered from Turek's destroyed reputation – her ex-husband had succeeded in obtaining an injunction in November 2007 placing their children in his custody to protect them from Turek. She was only allowed four hours with them in a week, and they always asked her why they could no longer live with her.

Another testimony cast doubt on Lucia's words, however, and painted her about-face in a sinister light. Klára's former friend Marcela Zednickova had also been friends with Lucia and had listened to her accounts of abuse at Turek's hands during their relationship. The change in Lucia's story had taken her completely by surprise, but she had a possible explanation – shortly after Turek was named as a suspect in Jakub and Ondrej's abuse, Lucia had come to her and begged her to talk to no one about the divorce or anything she had confided about her treatment at his hands. There were secret agencies at work, Lucia said, and Marcela had been warned not to look too deeply into the matter.

The Barbora question

The aspect of the case that was the source of the most controversy was what role Barbora Škrlová had played in the abuse. Ever since it was discovered that Ana had never existed, but had been a role played by Barbora, the question on everyone's mind was whether she had been a willing participant or a coerced victim herself.

Klára could not speculate on the question – she had operated wholly under the belief that Ana was Ana and had never been party to any of the machinations of the deception. But Ana had never been subjected to the same abuse as the boys, and had on occasion assisted and administered it herself, such as the instance of her holding Ondrej's head underwater. Jakub had been forced to watch that happen, and his testimony, which was read to the court, stated that there had been no reluctance to do the deed on Ana's part.

From the horse's mouth

Barbora's testimony painted a different picture. She reiterated that she had been forced into the role of Ana, and that Kateřina had threatened that she would be drowned herself if she did not do it to Ondrej. She provided more detail about how she had been forced into the transformation. It had begun four or five years before her adoption by Klára, she said, during which time her contact with the outside world had slowly been cut until the only figures in her life were Kateřina and Bašova. The process of transforming her physically had been extremely gruelling, she said – she was allowed almost no food, with the exception of one yoghurt per day.

Barbora claimed to have been subjected to physical sexual abuse by unknown individuals from the very beginning. The worst had been by Hansen, who had raped her and caused her bleeding and agony, all the while laughing and cursing at her.

The reason Barbora had been targeted was her vulnerability, argued her lawyer Richard Novak. She had always been physically and psychologically fragile. Her mother Renata provided the court with some details: since childhood she suffered from an enlarged thyroid, which had stunted her cognitive development, and had been diagnosed with epilepsy, proof of which was disclosed to the court by medical documents confirming the diagnosis.

As a result, Barbora had never been able to perform most basic adult duties on her own. She had always had to rely on other people, and since their time together in university, that person had been Kateřina.

Evidence to the contrary

Barbora presented the scars on her own body as evidence of having suffered abuse – cuts and welts she claimed had been administered by her torturers. Upon closer analysis, however, the marks told a different story. The welts – which she had claimed were the result of cigarettes being stubbed out on her body, as had happened to Jakub and Ondrej – were quickly identified as being ordinary abrasions. Their source was revealed when medical examiners noticed that they seemed to change position slightly the next time they were inspected a few days later. They oddly matched the back end of a pen in size. It was soon deduced that they had been self-inflicted.

The cuts were much older than she claimed and were actually the result of cosmetic surgery Barbora had had while in university – two symmetrical scars on her breasts were from a breast reduction, while several other marks on her abdomen were from liposuction. Finally, the medical examination revealed Barbora's allegations of having been raped to be a lie. There was not only no sign of physical trauma, but she was also found to have an intact hymen.

Psychiatrists' findings

Over the course of their incarceration, all of the defendants underwent psychiatric analysis. The experts who were enlisted to do the job were Blanka Zapletalová, a psychologist, Miluše Hamplová, a psychiatrist, and Růzeny Hajnová, a sexologist. Kateřina, Jan Škrla, and Hana Bašová had all refused to cooperate during all of their sessions, but good analysts are capable of needling the information they need out of a recalcitrant subject. The experts' findings were presented to the court on the tenth day of hearings.

The sibling dynamic

Klára was found to have histrionic personality disorder, characterised by a desire for external recognition and admiration, as well as a tendency to making excessive emotional displays. She also exhibited signs of dependent personality disorder, an inability to make decisions for herself without the approval of an authority figure.

Kateřina was intelligent, creative, self-confident, ambitious, and naturally authoritative, and Klára had naturally gravitated towards her for the approval she craved. But there was another side to Kateřina: she was also self-centred, socially distant, and lacking in empathy. These features of her personality had allowed her to identify her younger sister's lack of conviction and devise a plan that would take advantage of her for her own ends through emotional manipulation.

Klára was, in a sense, both victim and perpetrator. Ana had been perfectly packaged to appeal to her weaknesses, and the approval she received from Kateřina, the fictitious doctor, and Ana herself had become like a drug. She had fixated on it to the point that it drew away her love for her own children, and her maternal instinct had been diverted away from them and onto this one sick person. Blanka Zapletalová speculated that Ana had not even had to be a child for this to happen – Klára would likely have done the same for an adult, leaving open the possibility that even if she had testified untruthfully and had known about the duplicity all along, she would have followed down the same path.

Kateřina was also found to have sadistic and paedophilic sexual tendencies, which she had sated with her treatment of her own nephews, and likely extended to her manipulation of Klára's almost childlike nature. She had also actively participated in the sexualised "bonding" treatment that had been supposedly prescribed by the doctor for Ana. There was a possibility that she had had a pre-existing sexual relationship with Barbora – former members of her woodcraft club had testified about the two of them regularly spending hours alone in a tent.

Turek, Škrla and Bašová

Jan Turek was found to be emotionally unstable and exhibiting histrionic traits. He was impulsive and confident and showed an aggressive dominant streak. The fact that he had seemingly submitted to Kateřina's authority and obeyed her instruction during the abuse of Jakub and Ondrej spoke to a strong sense of hierarchy in their community.

Jan Škrla and Hana Bašova had been ruthlessly efficient in their uncooperativeness, but their silence revealed a great deal. The effectiveness of their recalcitrance came from very different underlying causes – Škrla's intelligence was below average, and his evasiveness was blunt and reflected his simplicity: he answered every question he was asked with an "I don't know" or "that's private." Bašova, on the other hand, was of above average intelligence and was more creative. She naturally gravitated towards a distorted view of reality and was better able to justify that view through use of her faculties. Škrla was also very attached to and thought very highly of his father, manifesting a tendency towards automatic obedience.

Barbora

Barbora, like Klára, was diagnosed with histrionic personal disorder, except her case was much more acute, manifesting in overt deceitfulness and a desire to manipulate others. She was not as defenceless or submissive as she pretended to be. During her evaluation, she acted infantile and vulnerable when it seemed to suit her, but when something was brought up that she did not agree with, she was capable of aggressively attacking it in a decidedly adult way. The personality disorder explained how she was so convincingly able to pass herself off as Ana and Adam – it gave her extraordinary acting abilities to the point that, in the moment, she was probably capable of convincing herself that she was whatever character she had taken on, and she could switch between different roles fluidly as it suited her.

Nevertheless, the decision to take on a character was deliberate every time. She evidently had not suffered any withdrawal symptoms from the drug regimen she had supposedly been forced to take, and neither did she show any sign of post-traumatic stress disorder like Jakub and Ondrej did. Her mind told the same story as her body – it bore none of the scars that would have been plainly evident if she had suffered any of the trauma she claimed to have.

As part of Barbora's defence, her lawyer Richard Novak had procured the aid of psychiatric experts of his own. Ivan Weinberger and Jana Telcová took to the stand to present their findings, and they were very different from those of the prosecution's experts. They stated that she did suffer from post-traumatic stress disorder – she was especially fearful of court appearances, they said, because she would have to be handcuffed each time, and handcuffs reminded her of her past traumatic experiences.

The report also contested the assertion that Barbora was manipulative. She was the very opposite, it said, and was naturally submissive and had a tendency to subordinate herself to authority. From her university years onward, that authority had been Kateřina, likely inspired by the splinter sect and, similar to what the prosecution's psychiatrists stated had happened to Klára, Kateřina had recognised that submissiveness and taken advantage of it.

Barbora had been used and abused and had her dignity destroyed and devastated, contended Telcová . A reprehensible experiment had been conducted on her mind, and it had left her with lasting and permanent damage to her entire sense of self. Yet she still exhibited some attachment to the very people who had abused her – the hallmark of Stockholm syndrome.

In addition to all this, the report brought up her pre-existing health problems – her having been diagnosed with epilepsy and the thyroid and liver problems, all of which had rendered her wholly dependent on other people her entire life. Imprisonment would be cruel and inappropriate for her, it argued. The best outcome would be for her to receive protective institutional treatment to help her deal with and erase the worst of the damage that had been done to her and hopefully help her become well enough to be reintegrated into society.

Professional differences

The polar disparity between the prosecution and defence experts' findings caused a near-uproar in the court. Trial judge Pavel Göth went so far as to ask the defence experts about the purity of their motives in preparing their report – an unconventional move – and direly warned them of the consequences of perjury. Weinberger and Telcová stood their ground. When asked about how Barbora had managed to fit herself into the role of Adam within a few weeks, when becoming Ana had supposedly taken years of conditioning, their answer was that she had been motivated by raw fear. She had been told that the evil people who had done her such harm were after her, and that she had to become Adam in order to evade them.

Both sides' experts soon devolved into flinging accusations of incompetency and ulterior motives. Rather than move the trial into its closing stages right then, Pavel Göth announced that the case would be adjourned for two and a half months, to reopen in mid-October. During that time, a new set of experts uninfluenced by either the prosecution or the defence would evaluate Barbora in order to arrive as close as possible to a definitive report.

Chapter 5 – The trial, continued

The trial reopened according to schedule on the 16th October 2008. Among the first orders of business was testimony that shed light on one of the mysteries that remained. Martin and Helena Fahrner took to the witness stand to recount how he had met Barbora and what had occurred until her arrest in Norway.

The vanishing act explained

Fahrner stated that he had known Barbora for a decade since his time with the Mravenci, but had only seen her very rarely, and not at all within the past few years. In May the previous year, she had turned up at his family's home in Šumperk, an hour and a half's road journey from Brno, in the company of two men, one of whom was Jan Tesař, another former member of the Mravenci. She had appeared extremely fearful and was in a bad physical condition, often fainting from the apparent strain she was bearing.

Helena described the situation they were faced with in military terms – *"Přirovnala bych to k situaci, jako když vám ve válce na dveře zaklepe partyzán a vy se musíte rozhodnout, jestli ho schováte"* ["I'd compare this to the war time; when a partisan knocks on your door and you have to decide to hide him in your house or not"]. Ultimately, they decided to take her in, thinking they were helping someone in need. Barbora had lived with them at their home for a while before departing via Poland for Sweden with Helena and the rest of the family while Fahrner remained behind.

Fahrner had followed fourteen days later, and in Sweden had met with Josef Škrla, who told him the reason his family had been dragged into helping Barbora was to wait for the media storm in the Czech Republic to calm down so that she could return without facing immediate backlash.

Fahrner stated that he had not been party to Barbora's first attempt at repatriation, but when it became evident that the Czech legal system's reaction to her return was going to be less than friendly, she had been returned to their care. He and his family wanted to move on to Norway, and Barbora had to come with them. She had to blend in somehow, though, and she had come up with an idea – to pretend to be Adam to throw off any pursuers.

What followed was a story now familiar to the court: Barbora had begun to take over the family's life. The Fahrners at first attempted to talk her out of her idea, citing the risk of discovery and danger that it would expose their family to. They had at first stood their ground against her protestations, but her psychological health seemed to deteriorate the more they resisted her. Eventually, they acquiesced, and she took to her new role with gusto. So that she could get used to it, she insisted the entire family call her Adam all the time.

The transformation had taken place before the family moved to Norway, and they crossed the border from Sweden with Barbora as Adam without immigration officials seeing a hint of anything out of place. As they attempted to settle in to life in Norway, Barbora had begun to chafe at her isolation. She needed a social outlet, she said, and the Fahrner's three children were not sufficient. She wanted to go to school as Adam in order to satisfy her need.

Again, the Fahrners attempted to talk her out of it, but her will proved stronger, and they ultimately complied. Helena had begun to fear for her very sanity – Barbora was so demanding that she felt herself beginning to lose touch with her own children. Fearing she would end up like Klára, so absorbed by Barbora that she would begin abusing her own children, she decided to take them with her back to the Czech Republic. Fahrner remained behind and tried to manage Barbora as best as he could – until her made-up stories caused him to be thrown in jail and eventually blew the lid off the entire deception.

In addition to the emotional, psychological, and reputational cost the Fahrners had paid, Barbora's intrusion into their life cost them financially. While in Norway, they had needed just one 200 kronor card between them for their mobile phones for a whole month, but Barbora blew through one every week or so. All told, they had spent 150,000 Czech Koruna helping Barbora evade capture – worth almost 5000 pounds in today's money.

Kateřina breaks her silence

The other testimony heard when the trial reopened was that of Kateřina. Prior to then, her engagement with the court had been minimal. Aside from short statements that Kateřina's and Barbora's testimonies were untrue and occasional interjected questions to other witnesses, she had largely kept silent. Whenever anyone attempted to draw her further, she declined, stating that she did not wish to incriminate herself or her loved ones.

Now, though, she had prepared a statement, which she wished to read before the court. The reason she had been silent this whole time, she said, was the difficult situation she had been placed in. Two people who were dearest to her – one being Klára, whom she had always and still loved as a sister, the other being Barbora, with whom she had lived a decade and looked after and cared for like a child – stood at odds with each other. However, when the accusation that Barbora had deliberately manipulated Klára became viewed almost as a foregone conclusion, she could no longer remain quiet.

Kateřina said that she had met Barbora in 1996. She recounted the problems Barbora faced with navigating everyday life – locking herself out of her apartment and forgetting that she had the bath running until it had overflowed and flooded the entire bathroom were common occurrences. Vacuuming a single room took her three hours. The cause of her problems was that she could not appraise situations realistically – her perception of reality was different from most people's, and she had trouble with both understanding and being understood by others.

Barbora had always been in need of another person to ground her, Kateřina said. Her relationship with her mother, who was an alcoholic and often neglectful, could not provide that for her. As a result, she had always turned to friends, going so far as to emulate their style of dress. Kateřina said that she had done her best to take care of Barbora and provide for her the grounding she needed. In 2003, she had turned to a specialist to provide therapy for Barbora. This is what she claimed was the source of the stories of brainwashing and abuse – due to her skewed perception of reality, Barbora unintentionally exaggerated things that happened to her six times over. The medication prescribed to her became constant drugging in her mind, and behavioural exercises seemed like torture.

In early 2005, Barbora met with Klára in Kateřina's apartment. Klára had failed to recognise Barbora, Kateřina claimed, and Barbora had unintentionally projected an image of being much younger than she was. This had provided Kateřina with a solution for taking care of Barbora – she would pretend to be a child, and Kateřina would have Klára to help take care of her.

Emotions boil over

Klára had been listening to her sister's statement in silence, but she could hold herself no more.

"Proč jsi mně to zničila?" ["Why did you have to ruin it?"] She burst out screaming. "Proč jsi mně to vzala, já to chci zpátky, proč lžeš? Ty to nevidíš, žes mi vzala děti? Já je chci zpátky!" ["Why did you have to take it away from me? I want it all back! Why are you lying? Can't you see you took away my children? I want them back!"] She collapsed in tears, and after her attorney spoke with her briefly requested to be excused from the courtroom. As she was being escorted out, Kateřina called out after her, "Já to chci uvést, jak to bylo, abys

85

věděla, že jsem ti nechtěla ublížit" ["I want to say it exactly as it was. So you'd understand that I didn't want to hurt you"].

After Klára left, Kateřina continued with her statement. In the summer of 2006, she and Klára had, with the help of "a man in whom [they] had implicit trust," devised a program for "re-educating" Jakub and Ondrej, who were becoming unruly. That was the entire purpose of all that had happened thereafter, she claimed. The supposed religious connection everyone saw was purely circumstantial. Barbora had played no part in the "re-education," with the exception of the drowning of Ondrej, which, as she had testified herself, she had been coerced into, with the threat of receiving the treatment herself. With the end of her testimony, Kateřina declined to answer any further questions.

A third opinion

The task of analysing Barbora and preparing the final psychiatric report had fallen to no less than eight specialists from the Motol University Hospital in Prague. Their findings were presented on the 20th October, the second-to-last day of the trial.

Unfortunately for Barbora, their report was not much different from the prosecution's. They found no trace of serious mental illness in her – the previous diagnosis of histrionic personality disorder stood but was joined by one of dissociative disorder, which manifests itself through breakdowns in identity, awareness, memory, and perception. Another, extreme symptom of dissociative disorder is cramps that seize the whole body as the mind loses its grip on it, and these cramps can appear on the surface very similar to epileptic seizures.

Finally, the report stated that Barbora had knowingly and purposefully taken on the different roles she had occupied. *"Nyní se sama posouvá do role manipulované oběti"* ["She is deliberately taking on the role of a victim of manipulation"], it concluded. *"Jde ale o účelové tvrzení, stejně tak její naivita je účelová"* ["It is an intentional claim. Her pretention of naivety is also deliberate"].

Closing statements

With the presentation of the psychiatric report's findings, the case was finally ready to close. A few of the defence attorneys attempted to request for further witnesses to be subpoenaed, but Göth declined, stating that no further testimony or evidence was required to decide the case. All that remained was for the prosecution and defence to present their closing arguments and for the defendants themselves to exercise their right to the final word.

From the prosecution

Prosecutor Zuzana Zamaravcová put forward the argument that the evidence and testimony that had been heard should leave no doubt that all of the accused had participated in the torture of Jakub and Ondrej. She specifically touched on the roles of the three main players in the matter: being a victim of manipulation was no excuse for Klára – whatever the reasons behind it, she had gravely failed in her duty as a mother. Zamaravcová was slightly lenient on her, however – her testimony had helped bring the other defendants to justice.

Kateřina's claim to have herself been a victim of manipulation by the mysterious "doctor" was bogus – she was far too confident and authoritative to have done anything without having driven herself into it on some level. Besides, all of the communications supposedly received from the doctor had been traced back to a phone number and email addresses belonging to her.

As for Barbora, Zamaravcová argued that her every action had been deliberate and self-motivated as well. She had played every role – especially that of Adam – while retaining agency and personal identity.

Because of the extreme severity and systematic nature of what had been done to Jakub and Ondrej, Zamaravcová proposed for the Mauerová sisters and Barbora to receive the maximum sentences possible – ten years each for the sisters and seven for Barbora. For the other three suspects, she recommended moderate sentences but left the precise decision up to the judge. In addition to jail time, she also recommended that the defendants pay damages to Jakub and Ondrej – 240,000 Koruna for the elder brother and 320,000 for the younger, at the time worth about 6,000 and 8,000 pounds respectively.

From the defence

Klára's attorney, Daniel Cevcik, argued for leniency for his client, highlighting the fact that she was the only one who had expressed sincere regret for her actions and had cooperated in revealing the full extent of the crimes. Even the prosecution's psychiatric experts had called her both perpetrator and victim. The main culprits were Kateřina and Barbora, who had deliberately deceived her and convinced her that her children were getting out of control. If it were not for them, she never would have committed the crime.

Even then, she had not performed the very worst of the torture, such as carving meat from Ondrej. She had simply been unable to force herself to do it. Her desire had been to set her children on the right path, and the reluctance with which she had participated showed that she still had some humanity remaining in her.

Turek's attorney, Milan Stanek, and Škrla's attorney, Zdenek Jaros, both argued that the testimony that implicated their clients was unreliable – Klára was the only one who definitively placed them at the cottage. Jaros argued that the only mention of his client by the boys was when Jakub stated that he brought him food once, and Stanek pointed out that the boys had only said that someone who *looked like* Turek had been at the cottage. Turek had led them in activities at the Paprška daycare centre for three years. If it actually had been him, Stanek argued, they would have been more assertive about identifying him.

Bašova's attorney, Libor Hlavak, stated that his client's role in the case was marginal and went so far as to call the allegations against her "stupid." Guilty or innocent, he argued, the media coverage of the case had been punishment enough for her. He requested that, if she were found guilty, she receive a wholly suspended sentence.

Two for the price of one

Kateřina's lawyer, Pavel Holub, spent more time defending Barbora than his own client. The entire trial had really been directed at establishing Barbora's guilt, he said, but Barbora lived in a world of her own. All she had ever desired from anyone else was motherly love. After speaking passionately on Barbora's behalf for thirty minutes, he finally mentioned his own client – admittedly, she had manipulated Klára, he said, but it had been done with the desire to provide a safe space for Barbora in which she could live the way she felt deep inside.

Škrlová's own lawyer, Richard Novak, made the final closing statement. Novak expressed his frustration about how Barbora had been handled by the law throughout the case. There were, in fact, two cases being examined in this trial, he said. The abuse of Jakub and Ondrej was the one that had been focused on, but there was also the abuse of Barbora herself. The latter had not had the necessary attention given to it. The assumption the court had held from the very beginning was that Barbora was guilty, and this had coloured every aspect of the trial. From the very moment she had landed from Norway – after, he pointed out, having given herself up to the Norwegian authorities – she had been escorted off the plane flanked by a pair of police officers as if she were a mass murderer. Ever since then, Novak had been trying to have her released on bail, only to be rebuffed each time.

Barbora's abuse had been ignored, he argued. He mentioned sixteen separate instances of Barbora being abused that had not been brought up at all. Witnesses he had requested be brought up to stand – including a woman who had seen her in a bloodied set of pyjamas and a taxi driver who had taken her to a therapy session. He also railed against Barbora's long-standing epilepsy diagnosis being suddenly overturned – an ailment for which she had been taking drugs with their own side effects.

Novak's final statement was directed at the public. *"Je to jen člověk, chce mít klid, nechtěla nikomu ublížovat. Ptejte se sami sebe, měla nějaký motiv dětem ublížovat?"* ["She is only a human being. She just wants to be left in peace, she doesn`t want to hurt anyone. Ask yourselves, what motive could she have to hurt the children?"] He implored. *"Pokud ji odsoudí, ptejte se proč?"* ["If she were to be found guilty, the question still remains: why?"]

Final words

After the attorneys' arguments, the defendants said their final words. Kateřina disputed the allegation that she had been the originator of the messages from the doctor, and stated that Zamaravcová had mischaracterised her claim about the role the doctor had played in her own actions. *"Ne tím, že tvrdím, že jsem byla osobou ovládanou"* ["I do not claim that I was being manipulated"], she said. *"Byla jsem ovlivněná, ne ovládaná"* ["I was influenced, not manipulated"].

Klára once again expressed her remorse for what had happened and stated that her objective had been to correct her children's paths. She made it clear that she was not asking for amnesty, but wanted to make it clear that without outside influence, none of the horror would ever have happened. *"Jen vím, že by se to nestalo, kdyby mě nepřesvědčili, že je Doktor, že je Anička"* ["All I know is none of this would have happened if they hadn't convinced me he was a doctor, that he was Anicka"], she said in closing.

Barbora was not present to deliver her final words, explaining that she feared being handcuffed and locked up in the small holding cell in the court building. Richard Novak read a statement from her. It alleged that the one definite instance in which she had committed physical harm to Ondrej – the drowning incident – had left her so scarred she had attempted to commit suicide, only being thwarted by the firm grip Klára had had on her handcuffs.

Jan Turek's final statement was a simple assertion that there were other factors at play, and that there was a need to investigate them further. Jan Škrla and Hana Bašova chose not to exercise their right to the final word, and in fact did not make an appearance at the courtroom on that day.

Verdicts and sentences

On the 24th October 2008, after three days' deliberation, Pavel Göth handed down his verdict on the Kuřim Case trial. After weighing all of the evidence and testimony, he found all of the defendants guilty of their respective charges.

To Kateřina, Göth handed the harshest sentence – ten years, in line with the prosecution's recommendation. The greatest incriminating factor was her apparent role as the instigator and organiser of the abuse of her nephews.

The fact that Klára had been manipulated the entire time did earn to some leniency for her. Her perversion of the role of mother was still a heinous crime, so her sentence was not reduced by much in relation to Kateřina's – she received nine years' imprisonment.

Hana Bašova and Jan Škrla both received seven years, while Jan Turek and Barbora Škrlová were put away for five. All of the sentences were to be carried out in maximum security prisons.

Unsolved mysteries and unanswered questions

While the conviction of Jakub and Ondrej's abusers brought a semblance of closure to the case, a great deal remained unknown. The testimony the instigators of the abuse – Kateřina and Barbora – had told rang hollow. The possibility of the abuse having been initiated for the purpose of producing child pornography was also more-or-less disqualified – the investigation had revealed no capacity for the large-scale production or dissemination of that kind of material, nor had examples of it surfaced anywhere outside of Klára's own home.

The involvement of Josef Škrla's Grail Movement splinter had been examined at nearly every point in the trial. Multiple current and former members of the sect had been brought in to testify, as had former members of the Mravenci scout troop. Their testimony had helped reveal some of the inner workings of the sect. Škrla had definitely used the Mravenci to recruit his following and had achieved this by slowly introducing spirituality into the group. Some members had resisted this and been ejected or left of their own accord, but many grew accustomed to the changes until they crossed the line into true believers. Škrla had taken several members with him to the Grail Movement's headquarters in Vomperberg, Austria to undergo the baptismal "sealing ceremony."

The members had developed a strong culture of secrecy and cooperation, but none of them admitted to having known about or deliberately played any part in the abuse, nor did they claim to know anything about a messianic plan. Those who showed signs of having cooperated – such as those who had falsified medical documents in their possession and those who had helped Barbora evade capture – reported that they had acted on that singular part alone without any knowledge of a larger plan in play.

The way everything had fit together strongly suggested an individual or a small, select cabal of insiders pulling the strings. The person to whom all indications pointed was the mastermind, Josef Škrla himself. His position as head of the sect, coupled with his mysterious transnational connections, would have been excellent tools for him to wield influence from the background.

Since Denmark, though, no one had any idea where Škrla could be. At the beginning of the trial, prosecution and defence had agreed that the trial could commence without his presence. As the defence had run out of strategies, however, they banded together and attempted to have Judge Holub issue a summons for him. Holub pointed out, however, that without knowledge of Škrla's whereabouts, there would be no way to compel him to answer the summons, rendering it a waste of time and resources.

Some still held hope that Škrla would surface on his own. The only time he had raised his head previously had been to help his daughter, and it was hoped that her facing prosecution would compel him to make an appearance. The entire trial had, however, passed by without a peep from Škrla.

Following the closing of the trial, the unit for uncovering organised crime launched an investigation into whether there were any other abusers involved. Part of their search involved attempting to find Josef Škrla. After nearly four months of searching, however, they found no trace of him and, satisfied that he had at least not been directly involved in the abuse of the boys, suspended their search.

If Škrla had been the inspiration and the organizer behind the abuse, he would go unpunished. Nevertheless, everyone could rest assured knowing one thing: that those who had done direct, personal harm to Jakub and Ondrej had received their punishment, and a semblance of justice had been served.

Conclusion – The aftermath

The Kuřim Case left behind ripple effects both in the lives of those who had been directly involved in it and in the psyche of the Czech people as a whole.

The media coverage of the trial was unprecedented, and no other matter has so thoroughly captured the entire Czech Republic's attention since. Every time events had been at their hottest – moments such as the discovery of the abuse, the fiascos with Barbora, and the trial itself – news coverage had been almost constant, with the case making the top story of every bulletin and the front page of every newspaper. Whenever things cooled down and news slowed down to a trickle, outlets continued putting out opinion pieces, interviews, and occasional check-ups on Jakub and Ondrej.

The media's appetite had, at one point, caused it to cross a line. Very early on in the case, just days after the abuse was uncovered, some of the footage of Ondrej in the closet somehow leaked out to the public. The source of the leak was never discovered, but when the media got their hands on the footage, television stations broadcast the footage completely uncensored.

This was forbidden by Czech law, which states that television stations have an obligation: "Bezdůvodně nezobrazovat osoby umírající nebo vystavené těžkému tělesnému nebo duševnímu utrpení způsobem snižujícím lidskou důstojnost" ["It is unjustifiable to broadcast images of people dying or people suffering from physical and/or mental abuse in a manner contrary to human dignity"]. For breaking this directive, broadcaster Prima TV received a fine of 900,000 Koruna (then worth about £22,500), while the stations TV NOVA and Česká Televize were fined 600,000 and 200,000 Koruna (£15,000 and £5,000), respectively. All of the stations attempted to appeal the fines by arguing that showing the footage constituted part of their prerogative as disseminators of information and was protected by freedom of expression, but were overruled.

Association with the trial and the surrounding media scrutiny gave a few organisations trouble. In addition to the Institution in Brno, whose case against Barbora and Kateřina for tarnishing their reputation had been thrown out of court, the Paprška daycare centre came under intense scrutiny for the fact that five out of six of the abusers had worked for them, as had a few of the individuals who had provided them support.

Karel Kincl, head of the organisation that owned Paprška, was quick to point out that background checks of all of the abusers had turned up clean, and at the time of their employment, none of them had shown any tendency towards abuse. In addition, Kateřina had run the centre with near-complete autonomy and executive decision making power over her hires. None of the people associated with her worked at the daycare anymore, and Kincl made assurances that hiring practices would be heavily revised.

When the extent to which Kateřina had used the daycare for her purposes was revealed, the remaining management considered shutting down in response to the scrutiny. Parents of children who still attended there objected to this, though, and with this explicit statement of trust from their own customers, they shelved the decision. The centre's name had acquired too much negative baggage, though. In June 2008, Paprška changed its name to Sluníčko, which means "sunshine."

The mainstream Grail Movement also suffered greatly due to its former association with Josef Škrla. Since the very beginning of the case, the Movement's Czech leader, Jan Paduček, had had to issue vociferous denunciations of Škrla and his group. It was indeed true that Škrla had not been involved with the mainstream Movement in over a decade, but this was not of much consequence to the majority of the nation's public. Like their earlier association with Jan Dvorsky, the Grail Movement in the Czech Republic would have little choice but to live with the stigma of Škrla's acts.

Time, therapy, and tender patience was what Jakub needed to help them overcome the terror of their past, and it seemed to be working. The pathologies they had exhibited at the very beginning were slowly lessening in severity – their fear, distrust, and hostility towards each other and the world ebbing away as their relationship edged closer to normality. The path was not easy, though, nor was it linear. The media coverage of the case was one of the culprits for this. Caregivers tried their best to prevent them from being exposed to it, but the boys had to go to school, and they couldn't exert full control over that sphere. Children can be insensitive sometimes. Their schoolmates, who had seen Ondrej naked on TV, would occasionally mock Jakub and Ondrej. The odd newspaper featuring front-page pictures of their crying mother also slipped through to them.

Whenever these things happened, Jakub and Ondrej would either lash out or break down. The truth about the one person they had been trained to adore also hit them badly – when Ana escaped from the Institution, they had both become inconsolable for several days, and when she was revealed to have actually been some 34-year-old stranger all along, it set the progress they had made back by weeks.

However, they were getting better. They also had the overwhelming sympathy and support of practically the entire nation. Gifts for them poured in, and an anonymous donor twice sponsored them on summer trips to the Italian seaside to give them a change of surroundings and get their minds off events back home.

The boys' custody was not resolved until June 2011. Due to being unemployed, their father was deemed unable to adequately provide their care. Eliška Mauerová's perjury case had concluded with the judge deciding that her motives in falsely testifying about Ana's origin during the adoption procedure had not been malicious, and so she had only been required to make an admission of guilt and was not prosecuted. Thus cleared, she and Ladislav were awarded custody of the boys.

Part of the boys' therapy was to help them forgive the wrongs that had been done to them. This was a delicate process, and had not been attempted when they were younger out of fear they would begin to blame themselves for what had happened. As they grew older, however, they were deemed ready and began occasionally visiting their mother in jail. Their first meetings was rocky, but things had smoothed out with more time spent together.

In October 2013, Klára was released from prison, having served five years of her nine-year sentence. The rest of her sentence was suspended for four and a half years, an abnormally long probation period that would make sure that if she exhibited any criminal behaviour again, she would instantly be thrown right back in prison. Relations with the rest of her family had been improving as well, and her sister Gabriela provided her with a place to stay and helped her find a job as a secretary for an employment agency. Though she could interact with them more, she was not allowed to live with Jakub and Ondrej.

Klára's fellow convicts were mostly released earlier, though the details of their liberations never hit the news. In June 2014, Kateřina was set free, the last of them to be allowed out. Details about her were also sparse, but it appeared she had failed to rebuild the bridges with her family as Klára had.

And so, as of the writing of this book, the perpetrators of the abuse of Jakub and Ondrej all walk free again. Whether they all have been truly rehabilitated is something no one can be sure of. They will forever live in the shadow of their past actions – and considering that their victims will, too, this is rightfully so.

About the Author

Ryan Green is an author and freelance writer in his late thirties. He lives in Herefordshire, England with his wife, three children and two dogs. Outside of writing and spending time with his family, Ryan enjoys walking, reading and wind surfing.

Ryan is fascinated with History, Psychology, True Crime, Serial Killers and Organised Crime. In 2015, he finally started researching and writing his own work and at the end of the year he released his first book on Britain's most notorious serial killer – Harold Shipman.

His books are packed with facts, alternative considerations, and open mindedness. Ryan puts the reader in the perspective of those who lived and worked in proximity of his subjects.

Other Titles by Ryan Green

If you enjoyed reading "*The Kuřim Case*", you may like these other titles by Ryan Green:

Harold Shipman: The True Story of Britain's Most Notorious Serial Killer

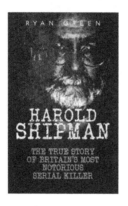

Harold Shipman abused his trust as a doctor and used his position to kill – no less than **218 of his patients** found their end at his hand, making him the United Kingdom's most prolific serial killer by a long shot.

This book tells Shipman's story, from his childhood under a domineering mother to his pathetic death in a prison cell.

We make a study of the man's possible motives and close with a look at the systemic failures that allowed him to kill and steps taken to make sure nothing like his murderous spree ever happens again.

Colombian Killers: The True Stories of the Three Most Prolific Serial Killers on Earth

Luis Alfredo Garavito, Pedro Alonzo Lopez, and **Daniel Camargo Barbosa** are among the most prolific serial killers in the world. Between them, they were convicted of 329 murders, but it's believed that the number they committed is **over 750**.

For these men, rape, and murder were but the beginning of the horrors they inflicted upon the world. The fear their crimes inspire is not about their nature, the methodology, or even the victims. It is about who the killers themselves are.

This book begins with three parts, each dedicated to one of these three monsters of modern-day Colombia. Once you've been edified with the general knowledge of the atrocities, we will delve further into the tiny details, the forgotten horrors, the thousands of ways that we as a society failed these men and, in so doing, shaped them into be the monsters they are known as today.

Fred & Rose West: Britain's Most Infamous Killer Couples

On the 24th of February 1994, police knocked on the door of an aging house in the English town of Gloucester. They'd come to serve a search warrant in the case of a missing girl – the daughter of the house's inhabitants. What they uncovered would shock the world: decades of child abuse, an underground torture chamber, and a burial ground containing the bodies of the spent victims of the torture – including that of the missing daughter. The address was 25 Cromwell Street, and these discoveries would earn it the moniker "The House of Horrors."

At the end of the investigation, the number of the murdered was twelve – all young females, including one daughter and one stepdaughter. The couple responsible were Rosemary and Frederick West, and this book will tell you their story.

Made in the USA
Monee, IL
18 December 2024

74325808R00059